Understanding and Affirming Autistic Clients

Understanding and Affirming Autistic Clients

A Primer for Mental Health Professionals

Chris Dabbs, PhD, HSPP, LMHC
Audrey Scaer, PhD

BLOOMSBURY ACADEMIC
NEW YORK • LONDON • OXFORD • NEW DELHI • SYDNEY

BLOOMSBURY ACADEMIC
Bloomsbury Publishing Inc, 1359 Broadway, New York, NY 10018, USA
Bloomsbury Publishing Plc, 50 Bedford Square, London, WC1B 3DP, UK
Bloomsbury Publishing Ireland, 29 Earlsfort Terrace, Dublin 2, D02 AY28, Ireland

First published in the United States of America 2025

Cover art by KC Koehne

A catalog record for this book is available from the Library of Congress.

ISBN: HB: 979-8-8818-0679-8
PB: 979-88818-0680-4
ePDF: 979-8-7651-5530-1
eBook: 979-8-8818-0681-1

Typeset by Deanta Global Publishing Services, Chennai, India

For product safety related questions contact productsafety@bloomsbury.com.

Brief Contents

Contents

Figures

Tables

Preface

Who Is This Book For?

We wrote this book to empower mental health professionals with the knowledge and tools to provide affirming, effective care to autistic clients. With this book, we aim to help you transform your clinical practice by integrating the latest research with practical strategies, fostering a deeper understanding of autism through an understanding of the neurodiversity paradigm. By reading this book, mental health clinicians and trainees will enhance their competence and confidence in supporting autistic individuals, ultimately contributing to a more inclusive and compassionate mental health field. Our promise is to inspire and equip practitioners to make a meaningful difference in the lives of their autistic clients and their communities.

Who Are We?

The authors acknowledge having differing levels of support needs from others in the autistic community. It should be noted that: (a) low support needs are often conflated with having no support needs, (b) support needs often fluctuate, (c) support need determinations are often a product of diagnostic clinician bias, and (d) support needs at any level are frequently societally unmet. That being said, the authors of this work acknowledge that autistic persons with significant support needs are often underrepresented within psychological literature (Stedman et al., 2018).

Similarly, we acknowledge that while we work within this text to provide resources for working with all autistic clients, the lens of our lived experiences likely centers on those with support needs similar to our own. Further, the content of this book is informed by our clinical practices, in which we work primarily with verbally fluent autistic adults without accompanying intellectual disability (ID). In attempting to decenter our own clinical biases, we invited professionals who work primarily with autistic children with varying emotional, linguistic, intellectual, and sensory support needs to contribute to this text—as can be seen in Chapter 3. We encourage readers to listen to the lived experiences of the autistic client in front of them primary to any resource or guide.

Why We Wrote This Book

Autism is one of the most misunderstood identities and diagnoses in all of mental health, which leads to negative impact on the well-being of autistic people (Turnock et al., 2022). Misunderstanding about autism is not limited to laity; clinicians self-evaluate as having minimal education on autism, including treatment and assessment competency (Lipinski, 2022). You may be thinking to yourself: "I am not one of these clinicians; I know my biases. I would never harm a client in this way."

We applaud your efforts and insight into your own practice, while also recognizing that many professionals hold biases and misunderstandings toward autistic clients: 57 percent of mental health professionals incorrectly answered that most autistic people have co-occurring intellectual disability, 53 percent incorrectly answered that most autistic people have special talents or abilities (i.e., are savants), and 73 percent incorrectly answered that autism was an emotional disorder (Lipinski, 2022). Implicit and explicit anti-autistic biases in the therapeutic relationship have been shown to decrease client self-esteem and act as a source of trauma for the autistic client (Darazsdi & Bialka, 2023). As with many identities and ways of being, we want to do our due diligence as clinicians to understand in order to best assist our clients. Your interest in this guide shows substantial investment in the well-being of your clients. Thank you for taking the time to grow and learn.

About This Book

Understanding and Affirming Autistic Clients is intended to be a broad introduction of important clinical considerations and advice for working with autistic clients. Beginning after Chapter 1 (which is where we encourage all readers to start), readers may pick up and flip to any chapter in the book for a relatively self-contained overview of the topic presented.

As you work through the book, you may find yourself interested in content beyond what we present here. For example, in reading about different ways of conceptualizing and understanding autism, you may find yourself interested in the disability rights movement. For this inevitability, we recommend digging deeper into our robust references and appendices, which may provide direction in your search for knowledge and understanding.

Finally, throughout this book, keep an eye out for infinity symbols (∞) which indicate a special aside or example! We hope this book provides you with a starting point on your journey of understanding the wonderful and broad spectrum of autism—you are an important part of changing our field to be more affirming and helpful for all brains.

The Importance of Specialized Care for Autistic People

Autistic people often experience a wide variety of mental health diagnoses—anxiety, depression, ADHD—at higher rates than allistic (non-autistic) populations (Lai et al., 2019). We explore this more in Chapter 5. The unique neurodevelopmental differences between autistic and allistic people can also mean that traditional psychotherapeutic approaches may be rendered less effective for an autistic client (Maddox et al., 2020). Specialized mental health treatment that recognizes nuanced needs and implements individualized approaches can be important for the well-being of autistic people. This specialized care can involve adaptations to standard treatments, communication strategies tailored to individual needs, and interventions that center on specific autism-related needs, such as sensory processing or social communication (Maddox et al., 2020). A personalized approach can lead to better therapeutic outcomes and improved quality of life for autistic people (Spain et al., 2018).

A Community Invitation

This book was written as a priming resource for autism and autism spectrum disorder for mental health professionals: social workers, professional counselors, school counselors, marriage and family therapists, psychiatric nurse practitioners, psychiatrists, psychologists, and any other (pre)-professionals interested in growing in competence regarding autism in the mental health fields. Because we truly believe in autistic-led research—nothing about us without us—we invite anyone reading this guide, especially those of you who are autistic, to send us your thoughts, critiques, or additions to chris@chrisdabbs.com.

Acknowledgments

We would like to thank Maggie Savage, M.S., CCC-SLP, for accepting our invitation to guest author Chapter 3, *Communication with Autistic Clients,* and Andrea Dell'Aquila, M.S., CCC-SLP, for providing insightful and thought-provoking questions as an early reader of the chapter. As expressed throughout this textbook, interdisciplinary care is vitally important in working with autistic individuals, and we value the perspectives that our speech-language pathologist colleagues bring into this space.

We would also like to thank Sam Miller and KC Koehne for contributing the artwork for this textbook, from the cover to the in-text illustrations. Follow Sam Miller on Instagram @shmugy for more of their amazing artwork.

We also thank Autistics Unmasked (AU), a non-profit organization dedicated to providing a safe space for autistic self-advocacy. AU is a diverse organization dedicated to amplifying and centering the voices of the Global Majority, queer voices, and the most minoritized. AU aims to provide an intersectional space for autistics to take control of the conversation around autism. Find them online at autisticsunmasked.org.

Finally, we thank Seth Kosanovich for contributing to the tireless (but not thankless!) job of source-checking this entire book. Thank you for keeping us on the American Psychological Association's good side.

∞

About the Authors

Chris Dabbs, PhD, grew up in Gary, Indiana. He, his wife, and their cat currently reside in Southern Alberta, where he teaches psychology, counseling, and practices as a testing psychologist. Dr. Dabbs is a licensed psychologist and licensed mental health counselor who is open about his own identity as an autistic clinician. In his research, he primarily focuses on ways in which social bias and stigma impact mental wellness, employment, and life satisfaction in religious minorities and people broadly described as neurodivergent. His research has been published in academic journals and collected volumes, and he has provided clinical training and presentations to national and local audiences. To stay up-to-date with his current endeavors, you can visit his website (chrisdabbs.com) or find him on all social media with the handle @dabbspsych.

Audrey Scaer, PhD, is an autistic psychologist living in East Michigan with a husband and a cat named Bubbles. Originally from Indiana, Audrey attended graduate school in Oklahoma before moving to reside closer to Lake Michigan and Cedar Point. Currently, Audrey works as a staff psychologist at Eastern Michigan University's counseling center, with a particular focus on working with college students exploring autistic identity, LGBTQ+ identity, or processing experiences of identity-based trauma. Outside of clinical work, Audrey collaborates with Chris on research focused on autistic wellbeing.

Maggie Savage, MS, CCC-SLP, is a pediatric speech-language pathologist who currently resides in Southern Alberta with her husband (Chris Dabbs) and their cat, Hermione. As a neurodivergent individual herself (ADHD and OCD), she makes it a point in her practice to provide neurodiversity-affirming care to her clients. She specializes in engaging autistic children in play-based language therapy, recognizing that all forms of communication are valid. Her other areas of focus include Augmentative and Alternative Communication (AAC), phonological disorders, and early childhood language development.

1

Understanding Autism and Autism Spectrum Disorder

Learning Outcomes

1. Understand helpful language regarding autism and neurodiversity.
2. Clarify different paradigms in understanding what autism is.
3. Interrogate what is meant by the "spectrum" of autism.
4. Debunk common myths and misconceptions related to autism and autism spectrum disorder.

Language Basics

Disclaimer: Community-preferred language changes quickly and should rarely supersede individually preferred language. When in doubt, ask your client what terminology/language they use for themselves and/or would be comfortable with you using with them. The following are some words and phrases that will be used throughout this text and are used in the autism literature. For a complete list of important terminology used in this text, please refer to the Glossary of terms.

Neurotype (noun): a specific type of brain (neurology). For example: an autistic neurotype, an ADHD neurotype, an obsessive-compulsive neurotype, a schizophrenic neurotype, etc.

Neurodiversity (noun): ". . . the reality that diverse minds and brain exist . . . ." (Dwyer, 2022, p. 1) A term that reflects the natural variation of neurotypes in a population. Describes a population, not an individual.

Neurodivergent (adjective): ". . . individuals with cognitive variation that is less typically occurring" (McConnell & Minshew, 2023).

Neurodiverse (adjective): description of a group of neurodiverse people. Most groups of people have some level of neurodiversity.

Autistic (adjective): A person whose neurodivergence is consistent with an autistic neurotype (McConnel & Minshew, 2023).

Neurotypical (adjective): A term for the majority neurotype in a given population.

Allistic (adjective): non-autistic, but not necessarily neurotypical. For example, someone with ADHD (and not autism) could be considered allistic and neurodivergent.

Identity-first language: referring to identity before personhood (e.g., "autistic person" vs. "person with autism").

Functional labels: e.g., "high-functioning" and "low-functioning"—clinically outdated labels that describe autistic individuals in relation to neurotypical standards of productivity and serve to diminish individual personhood.

Support needs: e.g., "higher" and "lower" support needs—describes the level of support that autistic individuals need. A term that should be applied to describe areas of need, rather than as a blanket description of an individual.

∞

Identity first language has been shown to be the majority preference in English-speaking countries amongst people with English as a first language (91%). However, in some international work, the opposite has been shown. For example, in a Dutch study (Bujisman et al., 2022), researchers found that 68.3 percent of their adult autistic sample preferred person-first language. The authors suggest that this could be cultural or related to the natural styling of the Dutch language. In an Australian sample (Bury et al., 2023), "person on the autism spectrum" was the most preferred term (alongside "autistic" and "autistic person"). Either way, we want to take client preference into account, especially for folks who may be English language learners.

Models of Understanding

The ways in which we think about autism are influenced by the philosophical and scientific theories and perspectives that inform what we think autism is. While there are a myriad of theories and discussion to be had about defining autism, there are two main perspectives for clinicians to understand: the Biomedical Model and the Social Identity Theory model. This guide begins with a discussion of the biomedical model, as it is the model of diagnostics and etiology that most clinicians are familiar with.

Medical Model

The medical model, also called the biomedical model, is a framework that practitioners utilize to understand and alleviate illness. Philosophically, this model begins with the presumption that all diseases and physical disorders have root in abnormalities in the body's physiological processes (Engel, 1977). Because the mechanism for disease is abnormality, then the remedy for the disease is removal of the abnormality. From within the biomedical model, if the root abnormality of the disease cannot be targeted, then treatment often includes symptom management.

For decades, clinicians had operated from the biomedical model in diagnosing and treating clients—until critics of the model introduced alternatives, such as the biopsychosocial model, with a stronger focus on a holistic understanding of health and disease. Even still, though, the biomedical and biopsychosocial models often fail to recognize important cultural and environmental aspects of psychopathology (Sue et al., 2021).

The most frequently utilized biomedical interpretation of autism for clinicians is Autism Spectrum Disorder (ASD), a diagnosis developed by the American Psychiatric Association (APA). Symptomatically, ASD is characterized by "persistent impairment in reciprocal social communication and social interaction and restricted, repetitive patterns of behavior, interests, or activities. These symptoms are present from early childhood and limit or impair everyday functioning" (APA, 2022, p. 60). Etiologically, ASD is seen as predominantly genetic from the biomedical model: "risk for the majority of cases appears to be polygenic, with perhaps hundreds of genetic loci making relatively small contributions."

Traditionally, because the "root cause" of the "impairment" of ASD cannot be addressed (genetics), treatment has often targeted "symptoms." Perhaps the most infamous symptom-targeting treatment modality is Applied Behavioral Analysis, which has an extremely storied history (Devita-Raeburn, 2016; see chapter 5).

We can see the philosophy underlying the biomedical understanding of autism through the language being used to describe people: "symptoms," "deficits," "impairment," "risk," "noncompliant," "resistance." The biomedical model positions autistic people as impaired, deficient, and in need of treatment to remedy their ailment. It centers what autistic people can't do.

Social Model

The social model of autism sits in stark contrast to the biomedical model discussed in the previous section. Instead of focusing on biological and physiological processes to understand autism, the social model emphasizes social, cultural, systemic, and ecological components. The social model of autism is subsumed under a wider umbrella of the social model of disability.

The social model of disability (Oliver, 2013; People with Disability Australia, n.d.) posits that disability is the result of interactions between people with differences and social structures that do not support their existence with these differences. In its most pure form, the social model of disability purports that disability is socially constructed. That is, disability arises, not from individual impairment, but from the "physical, attitudinal, communication, and social barriers" that prevent them from fully participating in society (People with Disability Australia, n.d.). Principles of the social model of disability include inclusivity, accessibility, equality, human rights, empowerment, and a focus on social change.

∞

Fernando is a seven-year-old autistic student struggling in his traditional first-grade classroom due to sensory overload and a rigid curriculum.

Medical Model	Social Model
Fernando is seen as "noncompliant" and "oppositional" with instruction due to his regular autism-linked meltdowns. He is referred to behavioral therapy to train him to quietly sit still throughout the day.	Fernando is seen as unsupported in his environment. His support team advocates for adjustments, such as a sensory-friendly classroom, flexible teaching methods, regular movement breaks, and a 1:1 paraprofessional.

Perhaps the most important component of the social model of autism for our work as clinicians is the inherent focal shift from client impairment to the barriers created by society that hinder our client's full participation. Understanding individual needs, and ways in which those needs are not being met by the systems surrounding our clients, is a vital first step in both advocating on behalf of our clients and empowering our client's self-advocacy abilities. According to Steven Kapp, a leading advocate in neurodiversity, "the neurodiversity movement begins with its goal of quality of life . . . and works backward from there to address the individual and social factors that interact to produce disability" (Kapp 2020, p. 7). This approach acknowledges individual difficulties present within disability (similar to early conceptions within the medical model), as well as positioning those differences within broader social frameworks.

Related, but distinct, from the social model of disability is Social Identity Theory (Tajfel & Turner, 1979), which suggests that individuals draw significant parts of their personal identities from the communities and groups to which they belong. Applied to autism, this theory focuses on the ways in which autistic people identify themselves as part of a group and how this group identification impacts behavior and self-concept. Results of current research suggest that meaning drawn from social group identity is the same between autistic and allistic people (Maitland et al., 2021), and that increases to autistic social identity are correlated with increased self-esteem in autistic people (Cooper et al., 2021). Throughout this text, you will see references to both "autism" and "ASD"—this difference in terminology is purposeful. We most often use the term "Autism Spectrum Disorder" or "ASD" when relaying data or discussing ASD from a medical model. In contrast, we use "autism" and "autistic identity" when discussing autism from a social model and Social Identity Theory perspective.

When applied to autism, social identity theory takes a neurodiversity approach, which views autism as a natural variation in human neurology and not a disease or disorder to be cured—similar to the social model of disability. From this neurodiversity approach, strengths and abilities associated with autism—for example, hyper-empathy, attention to detail, justice-focus, and systemizing skills—are highlighted. The strengths-based focus of social identity theory sits in opposition to the deficit-based approach of the biomedical model.

While the biomedical model has been instrumental in increasing our understanding of the biological aspects of autism, the social model (and related theories, such as social identity theory) can add to our understanding by providing a much broader and more holistic understanding of the experiences of autistic people through an emphasis on social and psychological contexts.

The Spectrum of Autism

Conventional interpretations of autism have characterized the neurotype on a linear, "low/high severity" binary. However, autism is much more complex than conventionality would allude. In reality, any two individuals diagnosed with Autism Spectrum Disorder may exhibit stark differences in behaviors, skills, and support needs. For example, one individual may struggle with understanding social niceties while another might have limited verbalizing abilities but show exceptional skills in music or spatial reasoning (American Psychological Association, 2022).

This autistic variability in needs also extends to the ways autistic people interact and perceive the world around them. Some autistic individuals might be extremely sensitive to sensory inputs—like sound, smells, or textures—while others might be under-responsive and sensory-seeking (Crane et al., 2009). These expressions of autism can also change over time through natural development, life experiences, and intervention, making autism a dynamic and non-linear spectrum.

The term spiky profile has been used to convey the complexity and non-linearity underlying the wide array of skills, experiences, and challenges associated with autism. Each autistic person has unique strengths and support needs, which are best understood through a personalized lens rather than a blanket "low/high severity" descriptor.

Each of these individuals has some similarities across their profiles—including social difficulty with neurotypical peers and mood symptoms. There are some obvious differences, too. For example, one individual has many more sensory needs than the other. This example highlights the heterogeneity of skills and needs in autistic people. Moreover, we can also begin to see a diversity of magnitude of needs between autistic people. That is, the depressive symptoms in one autistic person may be of a completely different magnitude and quality than the depressive symptoms in another autistic person. Understanding spiky profiles such as these can help clinicians engage more specifically with their client's unique needs. See examples of spiky profiles on the following figures: Figure 1.1 (a), (b), Figure 1.2 (a), (b) and Figure 1.3.

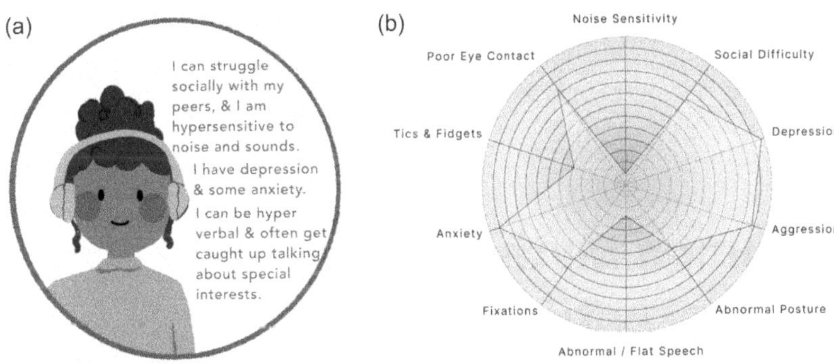

Figure 1.1 (a) Profile of a hypothetical autistic person and (b) "Spiky" profile indicating heterogeneous needs.

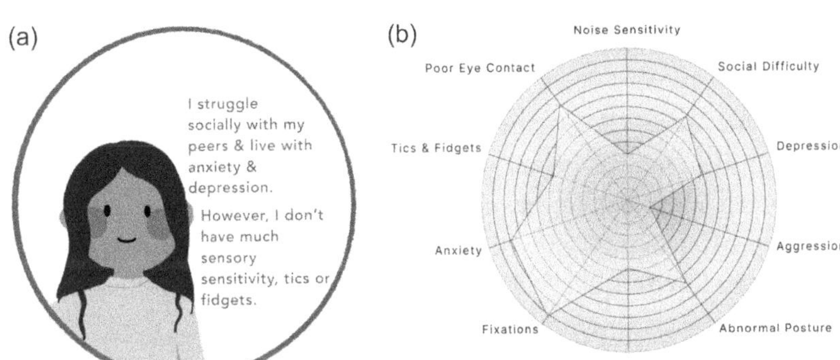

Figure 1.2 (a) Profile of a hypothetical autistic person and (b) "Spiky" profile indicating heterogeneous needs.

Figure 1.3 Autistic people are autistic, regardless of their differing support needs.

Common Myths and Misconceptions

Myths and misconceptions about autism abound. When analyzing our understanding of autism, it can be valuable to reflect on the sources that influenced our learning: movies, TV shows, celebrities, higher education, etc. In this section, we will engage in some autism mythbusting!

Myth 1: All Autistic People Have Savant Abilities.
Rebuttal: Most autistic people are not like Rain Man, nor do they show exceptional abilities in music, math, or memory. Savantism is quite rare, with approximately 10 percent of autistic people demonstrating savant-like abilities (Treffert, 2009). The worth and value of autistic people should not rely on the presence of such abilities or talents.

Myth 2: Autism is Caused by Poor Parenting or Vaccines.

Rebuttal: Throughout the history of ASD as a diagnosis, there has been speculation about parenting style causing autism (e.g., the myth of the "refrigerator mother") and autism being caused by vaccinations. These notions have been thoroughly debunked and there is no scientific evidence that parenting style or vaccine status impacts a diagnosis of ASD (Amaram, 2017; Rutter, 1978; Taylor et al., 2014).

Myth 3: Autistic People Do Not Want or Need Social Interaction or Friendship.
Rebuttal: It may be true that a commonly shared facet of autism is struggle with social communication and interaction with allistic people, but this does not equate to a lack of desire for social interaction in autistic people. Researchers have shown that, much like allistic people, autistic people who have a strong affiliation with their social autistic identity, and associate positive attributes with that identity, have improved self-esteem (Cooper et al., 2021).

Myth 4: Autistic People Cannot Feel or Express Emotions.
Rebuttal: A history of misunderstanding the behavior of autistic people has led to myths that they are unable to feel or express emotions or empathy. However, autistic people can and do feel and express a wide range of emotions. Some autistic people may communicate or experience their emotions in a different way, which can sometimes be misunderstood by allistic people who are not familiar with these differences (Dallman, 2024; Jaswal & Akhtar, 2019).

Myth 5: Autism Can Be "Cured."
Rebuttal: There is no "cure" for autism, and the concept of "cure" is often seen as controversial within the autism and autistic communities. Many autistic people see autism as a core, irrevocable part of their identity, not something that can (or should be) "cured." Instead, supports and interventions often aim to help autistic people manage challenges and enhance their inherent strengths (Kapp et al., 2013).

Myth 6: Only Boys Are Autistic.
Rebuttal: For many years, much of the way we understood autism (socially and clinically) was through the lens of the ways autism tends to manifest in young, White, cisgender boys. However, autism is not

limited to XY chromosomes, and people of all genders are autistic. While the traditional male-to-female ratio of autism is quoted around 4:1, recent research places that ratio closer to 3:4 (McCrossin, 2022). Specifically, these authors cite initial recognition and clinician diagnostic bias as some of the largest contributors to the disparity—not population prevalence.

Critical Thinking Questions

1. How could language usage play a role in rapport-building with autistic clients?
2. Compare and contrast the biomedical model and the social model of autism described in the chapter. How may utilization of each model impact intervention planning and conceptualization for autistic clients? What are the potential strengths and limitations of viewing autism through one model (i.e., unimodally) vs. an integrative model (i.e., multimodally)?
3. Myths such as "autistic people don't have empathy" and "autism can be cured" are still prevalent in society. How have common myths and misconceptions impacted your understanding of autism in the past? What strategies can clinicians and advocates use to actively dispel these myths, and how might doing so improve outcomes for autistic clients?

2

Recognizing and Assessing Autism

Learning Outcomes

1. Explore how the late diagnosis of autism spectrum disorder could impact a client.
2. Navigate fears, concerns, and biases in working with self-identified autistic clients.
3. Identify and explain the key reasons for the late identification of autism.
4. Critically assess the role of self-identification in the autism community.
5. Describe various screening and assessment tools for autism diagnosis.
6. Recognize and integrate cultural and social factors that influence the presentation, diagnosis, and intervention of autism.

Late Identification of Autism

Although research in autism spectrum disorder diagnostics suggests that accurate diagnosis can be made between the ages of eighteen and twenty-four months, ASD remains under-diagnosed in national and international samples (Brugha et al., 2011; Lord et al., 2006; Maenner et al., 2023).

Anecdotally, many late-identified autistic people even encounter mental health professionals for other reasons (discussed further in Chapter 5) multiple times before being identified as autistic—indicating a lack of clinical understanding of autism (Zwaigenbaum et al., 2015). Other reasons contributing to late identification of autism include sociodemographic factors (Mandell et al., 2002), gender differences (Lai et al., 2015), and diagnostic complexity (Lord, 2006). Prior to late identification, individuals experience feelings of difference, negative perceptions of others, and may mask or conceal aspects of their individuality (Kiehl et al., 2024). Whereas, diagnosis is largely associated with feelings of relief and clarity, alongside a period of re-understanding of the self (Kiehl et al., 2024). Because of the crisis of late identification of autism, many in the autistic community *self-identify* their autism before (or without) any professional intervention.

Self-Identification

Self-identification (self-ID) of autism, also referred to as self-recognition or self-diagnosis, is a topic of significant conversation in recent years. Many individuals identify as being autistic after extensive and thorough personal research, investigation, self-reflection, and recognition of traits and patterns of behavior consistent with autism. Proponents of self-ID, including the authors of this guide, argue that self-ID of autism can be an empowering and validating step that allows individuals to better understand themselves and connect with the larger autistic community, which has been mirrored within research findings (Bagatell, 2010; Routledge, 2024). Critics of self-ID raise concerns about the reliability of the practice and misunderstanding of diagnostics. Some worry that self-identified autistic individuals could strain already-taxed resources and services (Rosenblatt & Carbone, 2019).

However, research indicates that, especially when compared to allistics, autistic people have a much more realistic perception of autism—as both a lived experience and a scientific construct (Gillespie-Lynch, 2017). That is, autistic participants in this research were much less likely to engage in deficit-model explanations, held much less stigma, and were more aware of recent changes in diagnostics and scholarly understanding than allistic people. Also, research shows that some measures of autistic identity have the same validity for clinically diagnosed and self-identified autistic people (McDonald, 2020). Because of these realizations, researchers have encouraged incorporating autistic autobiographies into scientific research to refocus on what autistic people believe is important in diagnostics (Dinishak & Akhtar, 2022). Including autistic people in this research is a form of epistemic justice, as they have been often excluded. Our clinical position is that autistic self-identification is valid.

∞

A Case Study in Self-Identification

Cameron (they/she) is a transfeminine, nonbinary person living in a southern state in the United States. They have always felt different from other people and have trouble feeling understood by those around them. She experiences significant sensory concerns, has trouble when their plans change without warning, and has an intensive interest in reading, which has led her to their current career goal of becoming a librarian. One of their autistic friends, with whom they get along particularly well, suggests that Cameron look into autism for themself. Like the avid reader that they are, Cameron spends weeks immersed in reading books about autism and finally feels like they have a word for their experiences. Learning more about the experiences of other autistic nonbinary people even helps her to better understand her unique relationship to her gender (Voltaire et al., 2024). However, as a graduate student, Cameron does not have the funds to seek assessment services that are not covered by insurance. Additionally, Cameron is aware of recent legislative attempts in the United States to limit access to gender-affirming care for autistic adults. In the end, Cameron decides to self-identify as autistic, rather than seeking a formal diagnosis. This allows Cameron to become more immersed in the autistic community and to practice self-accommodation for her sensory needs.

Screening and Assessment Tools

Screening and assessment tools for ASD are essential instruments that help healthcare professionals identify and diagnose ASD in children, adolescents, and adults. Early detection, in particular, is crucial for initiating timely intervention and improving long-term outcomes. Evaluation for autism is an intricate process that makes use of screeners, questionnaires, assessments, clinical interviews, behavioral observations, and, often, collateral information from people outside of the client. These tools are often used together in an "autism assessment battery."

Some clinicians receive more training in testing and assessment than others. I (Chris) have training as both a counselor (at the master's level) and a psychologist (at the doctoral level), and I think the largest differences in my assessment training across those levels include advanced statistical and psychometric development training. However, you do not need to be a psychometrician or a statistician to incorporate ASD screening questionnaires into your everyday practice. In the following table, we list a few common ASD screeners and questionnaires that any trained practitioner can include in an intake appointment, alongside your PHQ-9, GAD-7, PCL-5, MDQ, CCAPS, and other standard screeners (Table 2.1).

This section is naturally biased toward the clientele that the authors tend to see in clinical practice: verbally fluent autistic adults. As many of these scales are self-report measures, they require a modicum of introspection that may not be appropriate for people of younger chronological or cognitive ages. For these individuals, we recommend assessments that often require specific training beyond familiarity with self-report measures. For example, the Autism Diagnostic Observation Schedule (ADOS-2) is a play and conversation-based diagnostic interview for ages twelve months to adulthood. The ADOS-2 has shown good clinical utility, and appropriate administration requires continuing education. However, I (Chris) have heard within my own community interactions that many autistic adults without co-occurring intellectual disabilities find the ADOS-2 to be infantilizing given the nature of the manipulatives (e.g., baby dolls, action figures, rubber ducks, etc.). So, while diagnostically valid, a clinician may want to consider an alternative assessment for verbally fluent adults with more age-appropriate manipulatives. One that I could recommend is the Monteiro Interview Guidelines for Diagnosing the Autism Spectrum (MIGDAS-2), one of the most neurodiversity-affirming trainings I have attended, which recommends age-neutral sensory manipulatives.

Table 2.1 Commonly Used Autism Diagnostic and Exploration Questionnaires

Scale Name	Release Year	Information
Ritvo Autism & Asperger Diagnostic Scale (RAADS-14)	2013[1]	• 14 items • Cutoff of 10 = 90% sensitivity[2] • Cutoff of 14 = 97% sensitivity[1]
Autism Quotient-10 (AQ-10)	2012[3]	• 10 items • Cutoff of 6 = 88% sensitivity • Some evidence cutoffs of 5 may be more appropriate for females[4]
Girls Questionnaire for Autism Spectrum Condition (GQ-ASC)	2020[5]	• 21 items • Modification of a questionnaire focused on autistic girls for adult autistic women • Cutoff of 57 = 80% sensitivity
Camouflaging Autistic Traits Questionnaire (CAT-Q)	2019[6]	• 25 items • Three subscales: compensation, masking, assimilation • Useful in identifying "high masking" autistics who may have gone unidentified
Toronto Alexithymia Scale (TAS-20)	1994[7]	• 20 items • Three subscales: difficulty identifying feelings, difficulty describing feelings, externally oriented thinking • Cutoff of 61
The Extreme Demand Avoidance Questionnaire for Adults (EDA-QA)	2018[8]	• 26 items • Cutoff of 45 = high levels of EDA (PDA)

[1] Erikson et al. (2013); [2] Sturm et al. (2024); [3] Allison et al. (2012); [4] Murray et al. (2019); [5] Brown et al. (2020); [6] Hull et al. (2019); [7] Babgy et al. (1994); [8] Egan et al. (2019)

For more information on specific tools and the role of evaluation in autism diagnosis, please see Chapters 4 and 5 of the Autistics Unmasked guide *Am I Autistic?* which can be freely downloaded from https://autistics-unmasked.dpdcart.com/.

The Role of Early Intervention

Early identification and intervention for autistic children are cornerstones in modern mental health care. These composite goals constitute a valuable approach that can dramatically affect the life trajectory of autistic individuals and their families. From the vantage of mental health professionals—psychologists, counselors, psychiatrists, social workers, family therapists, and so on—early intervention not only holds promise for improved developmental outcomes but also serves as a measure of prevention against exacerbation of potentially harmful symptoms and related mental health issues.

Early intervention can take many forms: speech therapy, occupational therapy, mental health therapy, and social skills programs. These methods have been supported in promoting social communication, sensory integration, increasing self-efficacy, and enhancing adaptive skills (Case-Smith & Arbesman, 2008; Paul et al., 2013). Importantly, some of these interventions target not just the autistic person but their family, equipping family members with skills and knowledge to support their child's development effectively.

When intervention is implemented at a young age, the brain is more plastic and adaptable. These malleable neural structures allow for the mitigation of potential developmental delays and the fostering of helpful skill sets. Early intervention is not a "cure" for autism—as autism is not a disease that needs curing—but it can set the foundation for lifelong learning and social engagement. From a mental health perspective, these early gains are not only developmental—they are intrinsically linked to psychological and holistic well-being. Improved social interaction and communication skills can lead to (a) better relationships, (b) higher quality of life, and (c) increased employment opportunities, all of which reduce the risk of associated mental health issues such as anxiety, social phobia, depression, and social withdrawal.

Mental health professionals play a critical role in the early diagnostic and intervention processes. They are often the first professionals to recognize signs of autism and can guide families through the challenging and complicated process of initial screening, diagnosis, and treatment planning. The involvement of mental health professionals is also instrumental in monitoring progress and making treatment adjustments to best center the needs of the client in question and ensure treatment comes from a neurodiversity-affirming and respectful model.

Cultural and Social Considerations

The history and legacy of autism research have predominantly centered on the experiences and presentations of young, White boys from Western countries. In fact, a large-scale review of autism research from 1990 to 2017 found that only 25 percent of studies reported race/ethnicity as a variable for their participants (Steinbrenner et al., 2022). However, autism is a neurotype that can occur in any person regardless of their sociocultural background—good autism assessment and intervention take this reality into consideration. Sociocultural factors not only influence how autism manifests, but also how it is understood and accepted within various communities.

In different cultures, social norms and expectations about behavior can vary wildly. For example, direct eye contact may be perceived very differently in Western vs. Eastern cultures. Cultural factors can affect how the characteristics of autism are expressed and observed, which may either mask or amplify certain traits. In a large, cross-cultural study, researchers found that autism characteristic expression differed in the domains of nonverbal communication, socialization, verbal communication, insistence on sameness, and restricted interests in samples of autistic people from Israel, South Korea, the United Kingdom, and the United States (Matson et al., 2011).

In the United States, these cultural and social differences in the presentation of autism have led to minoritized ethnic groups facing substantial barriers to diagnosis and early intervention due to linguistic differences, limited access to healthcare, or stigma associated with mental health. For example, Black and African American children are often diagnosed with autism much later in life than their White counterparts (Mandell, 2002). Similarly, women and girls are often diagnosed significantly later than boys and men (Gesi et al., 2021). Transgender and gender expansive autistic people experience clinicians lacking understanding of gender-affirming care and of autism, which at times leads to autism misdiagnosis (Bruce et al., 2023). This dearth of diagnosis, based on misunderstanding of nuanced sociocultural presentations of autism which impact assessment and evaluation, can and does result in missed opportunities for early intervention.

Familial and community relationships also impact how symptoms are interpreted and whether professional help is sought at all. Zuckerman and colleagues (2014) showed that social networks, including family, friends, and community, play a significant role in professional help-seeking behavior for the families of Latino autistic children. Communities that harbor higher levels of disability and mental health stigma may be less likely to seek professional help or present to professional help with more skepticism regarding the efficacy when compared to communities with lower levels of disability stigma.

Given these sociocultural realities, it is necessary for mental health professionals to be culturally sensitive and versed in the ways autism could manifest differently across social and cultural contexts. It is imperative that mental health professionals working with autistic clients stay abreast of current, culturally appropriate intervention strategies (Dubay et al., 2019).

Critical Thinking Questions

1. What might be the potential psychological and social impacts of late autism diagnosis on an individual? How may undiagnosed autism impact a person's self-concept?
2. Self-identification of autism has been presented as both empowering and controversial. How do you envision working with a client who has self-identified as autistic? What concerns or fears do you have in this area, and what role should mental health professionals play in validating or addressing self-identified autism?
3. How can mental health professionals ensure they are conducting culturally sensitive autism assessments? In what ways can cultural humility play a role in diagnosis and recognition of autism?

3

Communication with Autistic Clients

Maggie Savage, MS, CCC-SLP

Learning Outcomes

1. Understand and explain the Double Empathy Problem and how it affects communication in autistic/allistic dyads.
2. Develop comfort with asking and sharing communication preferences and needs.
3. Develop strategies to clarify and interpret client's communication patterns and intentions.
4. Understand how self-disclosure can assist in rapport-building.

Communicating with Speaking Autistic Clients

When communicating with autistic individuals, it is important to take into consideration the Double Empathy Problem. The Double Empathy Problem "refers to a breakdown in mutual understanding (that can happen between any two people) . . . more likely to occur when people of very differing dispositions attempt to interact" (Milton et al., 2022, p. 1901).

While breakdowns in understanding tend to occur between allistic and autistic individuals, it has been demonstrated that communication between autistic individuals is comparably effective to communication between allistic individuals (Crompton, Ropar, et al., 2020). Likewise, autistic individuals and allistic individuals appear to have higher rapport during interactions with individuals with a shared neurotype (Crompton, Sharp, et al., 2020). When aligned with this perspective, autistic and allistic communication styles are comparably neither better nor worse; rather, miscommunication occurs through differences between these styles. These findings are in sharp contrast to conceptions of autistic communication as having inherent *deficits.* In this framework, autistic individuals are seen instead as having communication *differences.* Implementation of this shift in perspective can help facilitate understanding, particularly in moments of communication breakdown. Without implementation of this perspective, the burden of understanding and adapting to allistic communication styles falls solely on the shoulders of the autistic individual to navigate.

Many of the differences between allistic and autistic communication preferences are rooted in approaches to social communication. Common differences are detailed within this chapter. To facilitate effective communication with one's client, it can be beneficial for practitioners to ask about their client's communication preferences, as well as share their own modes of communication. Not only does this allow for a greater understanding of one's clients, it also promotes clinician self-knowledge and acknowledges communication as a two-way street. Setting the stage with this framework also facilitates understanding and advocacy should moments of communication breakdown occur during sessions.

A more structured approach is recommended over an open-ended, subjective question such as "how do you like to communicate?" A structured approach can encourage more open discussion between client and provider, provide more information about how the provider can be a support within the session, and allow the client to get to know their provider. In turn, this discussion can establish rapport and trust. It should be noted that not every autistic person will have every commonly associated autistic communication preference. Many autistic people have a mix of both commonly autistic and allistic communication preferences. Similarly, not every allistic person may lean toward allistic preferences (e.g., a person may be uncomfortable with prolonged eye contact and allistic; Hammond, 2023).

Eye Contact

Many autistic individuals feel they can listen better without engaging in eye contact, as the effort to maintain eye contact can take up a high degree of cognitive focus. Some find eye contact incredibly uncomfortable or even painful (Hadjikhani et al., 2017). If forced to use eye contact, their ability to listen can also be greatly impacted. A client once remarked to me (Maggie), "Do people want me to make eye contact? Or do they want me to hear them? I can't do both at the same time." Many allistic individuals, on the other hand, view eye contact as a sign that their conversation partner is actively listening and can thus perceive lower levels of eye contact to be rude. In fact, recent research demonstrated that allistic individuals experience stress when their conversation partner is making low levels of eye contact, with no such finding occurring for autistic individuals (Clin et al., 2023). Autistic individuals may have different ways of demonstrating that they are listening, such as turning their body toward a speaker. Eye contact should never be forced with a client. Instead, a practitioner can ask their client how they feel they best listen and how they tend to demonstrate that they are listening. Some autistic individuals may utilize higher levels of eye contact than would be comfortable otherwise as an avenue for masking autistic traits (Hull et al., 2019). Given that masking can be both a conscious and unconscious process, autistic clients can also use therapy to explore what level of eye contact best facilitates their comfort within a non-judgmental environment.

Literal Language and Vocal Prosody

Autistics often value honest, efficient communication that is open and forthright. To allistics, this style of communication can feel blunt or abrupt, but it is not intended to be rude or disrespectful. In turn, autistic individuals may have difficulty when communication by allistics is vague or nebulous. Alongside this, many autistic individuals prefer more literal, precise communication, meaning that figurative language may need to be accompanied by additional explanation or context. This difference can also impact autistic individuals' ability to interpret differences in tone of voice (i.e., when someone uses sarcasm), as they often take and use words at face value. Conversely, some autistic individuals may not use vocal prosody when communicating to indicate changes in meaning in the same way as allistics. As a result, allistic individuals may misinterpret their tonality as monotonous. For example, allistic individuals may not understand when autistic individuals are portraying sarcasm in turn. Because of this, practitioners should familiarize themselves with their autistic client's specific vocal patterns and ask clarifying questions when necessary to ensure understanding of meaning.

Here, we provide an example of how this could present in a workplace. Alejandro, an autistic employee, and Jordan, an allistic manager, are having a one-on-one meeting to discuss a project that Alejandro has been working on:

Jordan: How's the project going?

Alejandro: The project's behind schedule because John didn't provide the data I requested last week. Can you talk to him about it?

Jordan: (*perceiving Alejandro's comment as blunt and blaming*) I see. Well, sometimes people get busy, and we all have to be patient and understanding. Have you thought about other ways to move the project along in the meantime?

Alejandro: (*perceiving Jordan's response as vague and not addressing the issue*) I don't understand what you're saying. I asked for data, and he didn't give me the data. We can't move forward without it. Can you help me get the data from John?

Jordan: (*sensing frustration but not understanding where it's coming from*) I mean, maybe you could try to work around it for now? Or find a different approach?

Alejandro: (*becoming more direct to seek clarity*) Are you saying you won't talk to John? I just need a straightforward answer.

Jordan: (*feeling the conversation is tense and misunderstanding Alex's directness as frustration or rudeness*) No, I didn't mean that. I just think we need to be flexible.

Alejandro: (*confused by the continued lack of direct response and figurative language like "be flexible"*) What does "be flexible" mean in this context? I'm asking if you can help with getting the data from John.

In this interaction, Alejandro is communicating in a straightforward and literal manner, seeking a direct answer to solve a specific problem. When Jordan provides an indirect response to the direct question, Alejandro becomes confused and repeats his question with clarity and precision. Jordan, on the other hand, is communicating in a manner that could be interpreted as vague and indirect, suggesting flexibility without directly addressing Alejandro's specific request. Jordan perceives Alejandro's direct communication style as blunt or potentially aggressive, not realizing that Alejandro's intent is simply to get a clear, actionable answer to his request.

Differences in Empathetic Expression

A common misconception is that autistic individuals broadly lack empathy. In reality, there appears to be a diversity of experiences with empathy among autistics, as may be the case within any neurotype (Kimber et al., 2023). Many autistic individuals experience high levels of empathy, or "hyper-empathy," to the extent that this can at times feel overwhelming to these individuals (Kimber et al., 2023). Other autistic individuals experience low levels of empathy which should not be stigmatized by practitioners (Kimber et al., 2023). Autistic individuals are more likely to have significantly higher emotional empathy (affectively experiencing the emotions of others) than cognitive empathy (recognizing and labeling the feelings of others) compared to allistic individuals (Shalev et al., 2022). In line with the Double Empathy Problem, for some autistic individuals, it is more difficult to empathetically relate to the experiences of non-autistic individuals when compared to others within the autistic community (Kimber et al., 2023). Given that measurements of cognitive empathy may be more reflective of an ability to recognize allistic emotional expression than autistic emotional expression, these findings together highlight the importance of further research to understand the nuanced complexity of autistic experiences with empathy.

Autistic individuals and allistic individuals can have differences in how they express empathy to others within interpersonal interactions. Oftentimes, autistic people show empathy by sharing an experience similar to what their communication partner is describing. This is intended to communicate understanding through shared experience. Whereas allistic people tend to mirror their communication partner's emotions to portray empathy. Breakdowns in communication can occur when allistics think autistics are "making a situation about themselves" by sharing a personal experience. Autistics, in turn can become confused by how sharing a similar experience to show they understand how their conversation partner is feeling could be seen as rude. For practitioners, this can also mean that self-disclosure may at times be an appropriate avenue to indicate their understanding of their autistic client's experiences when building rapport within the therapeutic alliance.

Monotropic Communication Style

The Monotropic Theory of autism conceptualizes autistic people as being clustered toward a narrow, systematizing, detail-oriented cognitive style (Murray, 2005). Whereas allistic individuals may view the whole picture prior to attending to the details, autistic individuals tend to build from small details to paint a full picture. This cognitive style influences numerous aspects of autistic experience, including communication patterns and preferences.

Allistic individuals utilize small talk as an avenue for relational communication through which the explicit meaning of what is said may be less important than the social function of the interaction (Coupland, 2003). For autistic individuals, a preference for explicit meaning may make the underlying function of small talk less intuitive and therefore feel less meaningful. Likewise, monotropic cognition lends itself to focused topics of interest rather than the more fleeting nature of small talk. This difference in preference for small talk can be perceived by allistics as a signal of broader social disengagement.

Autistic individuals have a preference to engage in conversation about topics that are meaningful to them for longer periods of time. These areas of interest are sometimes referred to as "special interests." Special interests can be a great area of comfort to an autistic person. In fact, according to the National Autistic Society, "Autistic people often report that the pursuit of such interests is fundamental to their wellbeing and happiness" (n.d., Intense Interests section, para. 4). For an autistic person, sharing about their interests can be a sign of relational comfort or a desire for closer connection. At the same time, allistic individuals may not understand why an autistic person wants to talk about something for long periods of time on repeated occasions, perhaps related to a preference among allistics for broader interests or social novelty. Within therapeutic settings, allistic clinicians may shift their communication styles depending on the preference of the client (e.g., not engaging in small talk on the walk from the waiting room to session) and allow the client to spend time in session sharing about topics of passion.

Differences in Language Usage Among Speaking Autistic Clients

Echolalia is a common language pattern among autistic individuals (Ryan et al., 2022). The root word "echo" within echolalia helps to illustrate its meaning. The American Speech-Language-Hearing Association (ASHA) defines echolalia as "repetition of utterances produced by others" (n.d., para. 1). There are two types of echolalia: immediate and delayed. Immediate echolalia is when an individual immediately repeats all or a portion of what they have just heard communicated to them (ASHA, n.d.). Immediate echolalia can serve a variety of purposes, including: (a) turn-taking: used to fill space/turn in conversational exchanges, (b) taking time to process information that has been said to them, and (c) a way to answer yes to a question (e.g., repeating "Do you want juice?" as a response to saying "yes" to wanting juice; Vicker, 1999). Delayed echolalia "refers to utterances that are repeated after a significant delay" (ASHA, n.d., para. 3). These delayed utterances can be something a client has heard hours, days, or weeks ago. Delayed echolalia serves a purpose in that the repeated utterances are often connected to meaning for the individual using them.

Individuals who utilize a great deal of delayed echolalia are known as gestalt language processors. A "gestalt" refers to a saved chunk of language a person uses. The Communication Development Center defines gestalt as, "the soundtrack of emotional experiences, and whenever you get to hear one . . . know that your child's first communicative intention is to relive that emotion—and share it!" (2022, para. 1).

∞

A Case Study in Gestalt Language Processing

Aiysha is a three-year-old autistic girl. Her favorite movie is *Toy Story*, and she has heard the phrase "to infinity and beyond!" many times. Aiysha has taken this chunk of language and uses it to communicate in other scenarios—like when she's running around, transitioning tasks, or wanting to go somewhere. This gestalt—to infinity and beyond—is being used to communicate an emotional or cognitive experience separate from the original usage of the quote. Individuals unfamiliar with Aiysha's gestalts may not understand the communicative intent of the gestalt, but we can teach them her language so they can help her get her needs met!

The above example centers on a child, but it is important to note that gestalts are utilized by people of all chronological ages. Over time, as gestalt processors engage in natural language acquisition, they will learn to mitigate gestalts or "mix and match" them with other gestalts. This allows them to eventually create spontaneous utterances. If a client currently uses gestalts, it is important to take note of which they use and what they mean to them. Checking in with guardians/caregivers can be helpful in this regard.

Communicating with Non-Speaking Autistics

It is important to note that just because an autistic individual is non-speaking does not mean they do not have knowledge of and ability to access language. Non-speaking autistics may use alternative and augmentative communication (AAC) to access language. AAC is an umbrella term encompassing several different modalities ranging from high to low tech. It is important to know the different modalities a client utilizes to facilitate communication. This section provides a brief, general overview of different options available to AAC users in the varying tiers. In reality, there are hundreds of different types of AAC devices. Therefore, it is important to build rapport with clients and create an environment in which they are comfortable using their AAC device within sessions. The more an autistic client communicates utilizing their form of AAC, the more a clinician can understand their methods of communication.

High Tech AAC

High tech AAC devices include digital devices like iPads, tablets, and other tech devices with voice features to verbalize for the individual. These devices may have pre-recorded phrases or individual words which the user can put together to form responses. There are several ways individuals can access their AAC programs, including by touch, via eye gaze, or via a switch. According to ESpecialNeeds.com, "Adaptive switches allow the physically challenged and special needs user to activate assistive technology devices in their environment" (n.d., para. 1). Switches can be accessed via touch (by hand,

Figure 3.1 Dr. Stephen Hawking was perhaps the most prominent high tech AAC user in modern history. Using a computerized hardware/software combination named ACAT (Assistive Context Aware Toolkit), an open-source platform by Intel Labs, Professor Hawking was able to verbalize when ALS left him unable to vocalize.

head, knee, elbow, foot), by mouth movements, by blowing in the air, or even through utilizing their tongue. Outside of these specific devices, individuals may also use talk-to-text apps or browser extensions to communicate.

Mid Tech AAC

Mid tech devices can include less complex technology than high tech devices. One common form of mid-tier AAC is BIGmack. A BIGmack is a type of switch that looks like a large button. A single message of up to two minutes in length can be recorded using a BIGmack. These recorded messages are often used by individuals to make requests, share information, or participate in activities. BIGmacks can also be used in play activities by connecting the device to an electronic toy. When connected, the toy moves when activated by pressing the BIGmack. Another mid tech AAC options includes the Go Talk by Attainment Company Inc., a communication board that allows the user to pre-record four to thirty-two messages with corresponding pictures.

Low/No Tech AAC

Low tech devices are categorized by their lack of electronic function. One example is picture communication boards, through which individuals point to picture/word representations to express themselves. Other low/no tech devices include communication binders full of pictures that can be pointed to, yes/no boards, and written responses.

AAC and Selective Mutism

It has been noted that while not all autistics experience selective mutism, among those with selective mutism autism is a common co-occurring diagnosis (Steffenburg et. al, 2018). Selective mutism is characterized by a "Consistent failure to speak in specific social situations in which there is an expectation of speaking . . . despite speaking in other situations" (American Psychological Association, 2022, p. 222). As a result, autistics who experience selective mutism may be part-time AAC users to facilitate communication when experiencing a period of selective mutism. If a client has not established a mode of AAC for times of experienced selective mutism, the client may not have clear avenues for communicating should this occur during therapy sessions. Asking clients about how they would like to communicate (writing, typing on a shared document, talk-to-text, etc.) can help facilitate communication and, hopefully, build rapport and trust in the therapeutic relationship. It is important to note that selective mutism and verbal shutdowns are separate, though related, constructs—read more about each of these in the Glossary of this text.

Building Rapport and Trust with Autistic Clients

Like with any client, building rapport and trust is an integral part of the therapeutic relationship. Utilizing the approach described within this chapter toward honoring an individual client's ways of communicating is one important avenue for establishing this trust. Through increasing rapport and trust, autistic clients can be their authentic selves within the session. Beyond communication needs, accommodating an autistic client's sensory needs can also help to encourage trust and feelings of safety in the therapy settings. Asking clients what may trigger dysregulation for them (e.g., light, sound, coming into session after a long day of cognitive demands) and how they can be supported in their internal regulation within session can help build trust. Having accommodations available like dimming lights, having fidgets in one's office, and allowing the client to move their body within the space rather than remaining still may all be helpful to the client. Without sensory accommodations, not only can the client feel discomforted within the session, but their ability to regulate their emotional responses can also be negatively impacted. All of this in turn can impact a client's ability to communicate. The key within this area is to allow the therapeutic setting to be a safe space for sensory regulation so the client does not have to mask their needs.

Building Rapport Using Social Stories

One specific avenue for increasing rapport and trust with autistic clients is through utilizing social stories. Social stories are narrative descriptions of everyday situations and events that illustrate desired social interactions in a clear and reassuring manner. Social stories, when created by neuro-affirming clinicians with the goal of strengthening social relational ability—not just autistic-allistic relations—can help autistic individuals better understand social norms and expectations, especially those that may be unvoiced or covert (Gray & Garand, 1993). Social stories can be used to help clients understand the trajectory of therapy, session expectations, and process their emotions, all of which can contain unvoiced or covert aspects. Vitally, social stories should not be used to elicit compliance or encourage masking. Rather, they should be used as a tool to alleviate anxiety and help the client place themselves into an unfamiliar scenario and understand it.

Building Rapport with PDA Clients

Persistent Drive for Autonomy, otherwise known as Pathological Demand Avoidance or PDA, has been considered a specific autistic profile marked by a strong preference for independence and coinciding protective strategies against external demands (PDA Society, 2022). Framing this constellation of experiences under the PDA label has been criticized by some autistic activists for pathologizing strategies by autistic individuals toward autonomy and agency (Milton, 2013). Simultaneously, some autistic individuals have found self-understanding and self-compassion through understanding themselves within this label. After all, underlying the avoidance of demands are often elevated, persistent levels of anxious distress (PDA Society, n.d.). In turn, a buildup of external demands can contribute to lability in mood (PDA Society, 2022).

Understanding the internal experiences of PDA may allow for better communication with autistic clients within this profile, as well as ensuring such clients are supported within therapy settings. For individuals with a PDA profile, a collaborative approach is of marked necessity for therapeutic success, as a hierarchical approach may not make sense intuitively to these individuals, and it could potentially serve to elevate rather than mitigate underlying anxious distress (PDA Society, 2022). Autistic individuals with a PDA profile may mask their autistic traits, meaning that social difficulties may not be as easily recognized earlier in treatment (PDA Society, 2022). Likewise, social strategies may be utilized in order to mitigate external demands (e.g., avoiding higher acuity topics of conversation in session through steering the conversation toward other topics) (PDA Society, 2022). Importantly, some aspects of communication can be experienced by the individual as an external demand. For instance, hidden within a direct question is a demand for a specific answer (PDA Society, 2022). Because of this, some autistic individuals within this profile may prefer questions or requests to be communicated less directly than to other autistic clients (PDA Society, 2022).

It should be acknowledged that this recommendation may feel seemingly contradictory to the general recommendation for direct communication to autistic persons within this chapter. In this way, the PDA profile of autism may serve as a point of reflection for practitioners on the importance of individualized communication approaches from client to client. Like any individual client, having a label for their neurotype may provide more information about a client's experiences, and the personhood of each individual plays a necessary role in understanding the interrelatedness of their experiences with their autistic identity.

Critical Thinking Questions

1. In what ways may utilizing the Double Empathy Problem as a framework for understanding autistic communication impact therapeutic interactions? How can clinicians apply this understanding to improve therapeutic communication with autistic clients?
2. How may a preference for direct communication among autistic clients differ from communication styles often emphasized in other therapeutic settings?
3. Some autistic clients, particularly those with a PDA profile, may require less direct communication, which contrasts with the typical recommendation for straightforward language. How can clinicians balance the need for individualized communication approaches with maintaining consistency in their therapeutic approach? What are your reactions and thoughts on the PDA profile of autism?

4

Understanding Autistic Mental Health Outcomes

Learning Outcomes

1. Recognize the complexity of dual diagnosis in autistic clients.
2. Understand the historical contexts affecting diagnosis of ADHD and ASD.
3. Identify the unique needs of autistic people with Intellectual Developmental Disorders.
4. Recognize the increased prevalence of addiction in autistic clients.

Co-Occurrence of Autism with Other Mental Health Concerns

Professionally diagnosed and self-diagnosed autistic individuals are more likely to have received a previous additional diagnosis by a mental health professional than allistic individuals (Au-Yeung et al., 2019). Simultaneously, professionally and self-diagnosed autistics are more likely to not fully agree with these diagnoses (Au-Yeung et al., 2019). They indicate previous clinicians either did not understand them or their autism, that clinicians ascribed autism-related experiences to other conditions, or that additional diagnoses were related to autism-specific stressors (Au-Yeung et al., 2018). In one study, about one-fourth of autistic adults perceived a previous diagnosis of another mental health condition as a misdiagnosis (Kentrou et al., 2024). Because of this, clinicians must both (1) recognize that autistic people face disproportionate negative mental health outcomes and (2) ensure they are not pathologizing autistic experiences due to misperceptions of autism. The goal of this chapter is to provide a starting point for recognizing this distinction in autistic clients.

Attention-Deficit/Hyperactivity Disorder

Autistic clients are more likely to experience co-occurring neurodiversity, including through co-occurring ADHD (sometimes referred to within the community as "AuDHD"). Though estimated rates differ by study, the most recent meta-analysis indicates a lifetime co-occurrence of ADHD among autistic individuals of 40.2 percent (Rong et al., 2021). Despite this high co-occurrence, prior to the release of the DSM-5 in 2013, both could not be diagnosed at the same time. Therefore, especially for clients who received a formal diagnosis prior to these changes, clinicians should be cognizant of the likelihood of missed diagnoses. For those who received a formal diagnosis subsequent to 2013, it is still worth exploring their specific diagnostic process. This is because formal assessment is often siloed between conditions, rather than assessing for both at once. For self-diagnosed clients, ADHD may be an avenue for additional self-exploration.

Both autistics and ADHDers experience differences in social communication and behaviors. Among ADHDers, social differences can be related to attentional differences and impulsivity (Sokolova et al., 2017). For instance, an ADHDer may engage in higher levels of conversational overlapping (or interruption) in relation to impulsivity, or not notice discomfort in their conversation partner because their attention is focused elsewhere. Among ADHDers, the resulting criticism by peers can impact well-being and self-worth (Beaton et al., 2022). Both ADHDers and autistics stim or fidget, but among ADHDers this may be more related to hyperactive energy (Sokolova et al., 2017). Individuals draw strengths from their ADHD, including viewing themselves as dynamic and creative, open to new experiences, prosocial and outgoing, and having unique cognitive strengths like the ability to hyperfocus (Schippers et al., 2022). In this way, clinicians should work to identify both concerns and strengths related to their client's unique experience of AuDHD.

Intellectual Developmental Disorders

Autistic people are more likely than the general population to have an accompanying intellectual disability, with some sources placing the co-occurrence of autism and ID at 31 percent (Baoi, 2018). It should be acknowledged that intelligence tests have been shown to often operate unexpectedly with autistic individuals. For example, Nader and colleagues (2016) research showed that the Wechsler Intelligence Scale for Children (WISC), one of the most widely used intelligence tests in autistic populations, significantly underestimates autistic intelligence. When these researchers compared autistic/allistic intelligence scores, allistic children scored equally across the WISC and another intelligence test (Raven's Progressive Matrices), while autistic children significantly underperformed on the WISC compared to Raven's.

Similarly, autistic individuals often have significant differences in cognitive abilities, not tied to their intelligence scores. In a study of autistic adolescents, Duncan & Bishop (2015) showed that about half of autistic individuals in this sample had daily living skills significantly below expectations for someone their age and IQ. The disconnect between IQ and adaptive skills can be a source of frustration for both autistic individuals and those in their support systems, as others may not understand why someone with high cognitive function (i.e., "book smarts") might struggle with daily living activities. The nuance in this conversation is helpfully reviewed in an article from the Kennedy Krieger Institute, a developmental and neurological support institute (Sarris, 2015). Autistic individuals with co-occurring intellectual disabilities have unique needs that deserve support and acknowledgment. These discrepancies highlight the challenges in accurately measuring intelligence in autistic individuals using traditional IQ tests.

When utilizing the DSM-5's support needs designation system, some evidence indicates a lower intelligence quotient score is associated with higher support needs determinations in social communication and repetitive behaviors (Mazurek et al., 2019). Autistic children with a co-occurring intellectual disability may be more likely than children without a co-occurring intellectual disability to have documented developmental delays, but less likely to be diagnosed with co-occurring developmental or psychiatric disorder (Etyemez et al., 2022). This could suggest, among other possibilities, underdiagnosis of mental health concerns among this population. In support of this possibility, nearly 30 percent of a sample of adults diagnosed with an intellectual disability had a missed diagnosis of a mental health concern, with the most common missed diagnoses being anxiety or depression (Peña-Salazar et al., 2020). Likewise, some research has found that autistic people with intellectual disability have greater symptoms of a variety of mental health concerns compared to individuals with solely a diagnosis of an intellectual disability (Cervantes & Matson, 2015). Clinicians working with autistic adults with co-occurring intellectual disability described PTSD symptoms among these clients as potentially more difficult to identify, especially with a lack of specific assessment instruments to utilize (Kildahl et al., 2020). The authors of this guide support ongoing research to better identify and provide support for the mental health needs of these members of the autistic community.

Depression

Autistic people are more likely to experience depression (Lugo-Marín et al., 2019). Alongside this, it is vital that clinicians recognize that this population is at increased risk for suicide, with a systematic review of 48,186 autistic and suspected autistic persons finding that over a third (34.2%) experienced suicidal ideation, 21.9 percent had made specific plans for suicide, and nearly a quarter (24.3%) had engaged in suicidal behaviors (Newell et al., 2023). Therefore, safety planning with this population is of the utmost importance. Among autistics experiencing depression, mastery, or perceived control over life stressors, is strongly associated with depressive symptoms (van Heijst et al., 2020). At the same time, depression is associated with social worries, financial worries, and worries about independence (van Heijst et al., 2019). Therefore, treatment of depression in autistic clients should emphasize empowerment inside and outside of session.

Generalized Anxiety

Autistic people are more likely to have elevated levels of anxiety (Ruzzano et al., 2015). It's important to recognize that this anxiety can be interrelated with autistic experience. For instance, autistic individuals may notice physical symptoms of anxiety (such as sweating, increasing heart rate, stomach pain, etc.) prior to noticing internal emotional signals (Halim et al., 2018). This may be interrelated with the commonality of alexithymia, or an internal difficulty recognizing emotions, among autistics (Kinnaird et al., 2019). Autistic individuals also experience anxiety in relation to sensory overload from the environment, in relation to schedule or plan changes, and in relation to executive functioning concerns (Halim et al., 2018). Preventing an autistic person from stimming also leads to increased

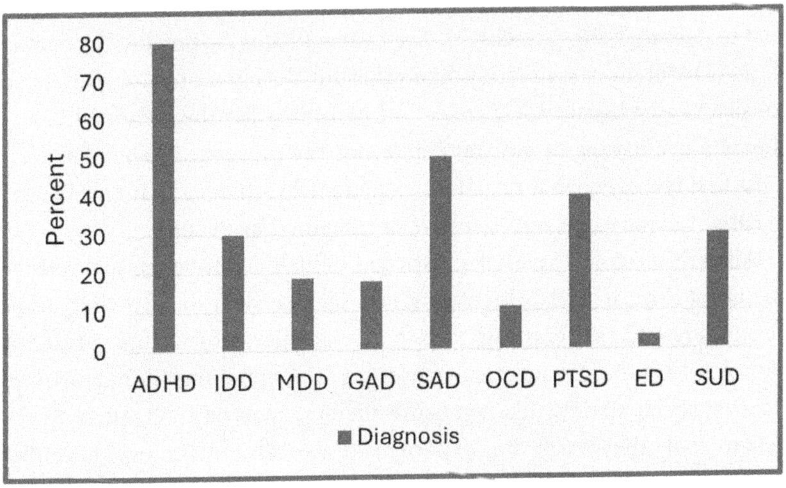

Figure 4.1 Prevalences of co-occurring mental health diagnoses in autistic people.

anxiety (Halim et al., 2020), as does camouflaging of autistic traits in general (Hull et al., 2021). While high levels of anxiety can result in a panic attack in autistic persons, it may also result in an autistic shutdown or meltdown (Halim et al., 2020). Clinicians should focus on increasing positive coping mechanisms for mindfulness or relaxation, while at the same time empowering clients to seek accommodations or self-accommodate for autistic needs that when unmet lead to anxiety. This could look like encouraging a client to carry fidget items, tinted glasses, or ear protection to meet sensory needs, or writing an accommodation letter for the client's workplace as requested.

Social Anxiety

Social Anxiety Disorder impacts autistic individuals at disproportionate rates (Maddox & White, 2015) The American Psychological Association (2022) indicates a key feature of this condition is an excessive fear of negative evaluation by others that does not match reality. It is up to the clinician to determine if these fears are excessive or not (American Psychological Association, 2022). Research also indicates that allistic individuals view autistic persons as less likable, less attractive, less dominant, and more awkward than allistic persons based on brief exposures (Sasson et al., 2017). Based on these exposures, allistics are also less likely to want to sit next to, talk to, hang out with, or live near said autistic persons (Sasson et al., 2017). Put more simply, it is likely that autistic clients have experienced consistent immediate social rejection by others for their entire lives. A clinician evaluating an autistic person for the presence of social anxiety must first recognize that negative evaluations by others are often a feature of autistic experience, not excessive or imagined by default.

All of this is not to say that autistic individuals cannot experience social anxiety at clinical levels. However, it is to say that such social anxiety must be understood as existing within social hierarchies that presently pathologize authentic autistic experiences. Therefore, traditional forms of treating social anxiety, like exposure therapy, may be inadequate to the extent that they may be experienced as retraumatizing. Likewise, cognitive-behavioral approaches may inappropriately attempt to reframe social fears, viewing them as "irrational" (Wilson, 2024). Instead, the reduction of social anxiety must include validation of what clients are experiencing and have experienced socially. Qualitative literature in this area identified that autistic individuals with social anxiety had negative core beliefs related to past experiences of social rejection (Spain et al., 2020). Processing these past experiences may be an avenue for increasing self-compassion, self-esteem, and self-efficacy. Alongside this, treatment must include validation of autistic communication styles by the therapist, as well as potentially empowering the client to seek community with other autistic individuals.

Obsessive-Compulsive and Related Disorders

Autism and Obsessive-Compulsive Disorder (OCD) are commonly co-occurring conditions (Meier et al., 2015). There is evidence of shared phenotypes and neurobiology of OCD with Autism and ADHD (Kushki et al., 2019). At the same time, clinicians must be aware that the nature of repetitive behaviors in autism and OCD is distinctive (Ruzzano et al., 2015). Among autistic people, repetitive behaviors are not associated with obsessive fears, as is characteristic of OCD (where repetitive compulsive behavior is utilized in response to said fears) (Ruzzano et al., 2015). Rather, repetitive behaviors like stimming or routines are forms of self-care and well-being among autistic persons (Long et al., 2024; Kapp et al., 2019). In autism, repetitive behaviors are ego-syntonic, or aligned with an individual's internal sense of personhood, whereas compulsive behaviors within OCD are ego-dystonic, or disarranged with an individual's sense of who they are (Cooper et al., 2024). In this way, clinicians must go beyond observing outward repetitive behaviors of autistic clients and instead learn about the internal experiences that those repetitive behaviors are related to.

Among autistic individuals with OCD, autism and OCD can intersect in their presentation (Cooper et al., 2024). For instance, OCD compulsive behaviors can intrude within autistic routines (Cooper et al., 2024). In turn, disruptions to both a routine and completion of a compulsion can feel even more distressing (Cooper et al., 2024). Given that special interests can be deeply tied to individual values, OCD intrusive thoughts can become entangled within special interests (Cooper et al., 2024). For instance, an autistic individual with a special interest in psychology may care deeply about understanding individuals. In turn, OCD obsessive thoughts may become centered on instances in which said person feels they have misunderstood others.

Clinicians should also consider the potential presence of clinical levels of body-focused repetitive behaviors (BFRBs) like trichotillomania (hair pulling) and excoriation (skin picking) among this population. While there is a need for more research in this area, among adolescents presenting for treatment of BFRBs, ADHD and autism were the most frequently reported co-occurring diagnoses (Rautio et al., 2023). Additionally, the rate of significant levels of autistic traits appears to be higher among those with trichotillomania (Grant & Chamberlain, 2022). In a population derived stratified sample of autistic children, the co-occurrence of trichotillomania was 3.9 percent, which appears to be higher than the rate among the general population (Simonoff et al., 2008). Within the DSM-5-TR, BFRBs are a diagnostic concern when individuals have tried repeatedly to reduce the behaviors with no success and when they are a source of distress for the individual (APA, 2022).

Simultaneously, BFRBs can be a form of stimming among autistic clients (Kapp et al., 2019). Autistic individuals describe forms of stimming that can cause personal harm, as well as stimming behaviors that lead to no personal harm but which are stigmatized by others (Kapp et al., 2019). Since stimming is such an important aspect of self-regulation for autistic clients, it is important that clinicians take the client's lead regarding their perceptions of stimming behaviors. For example, cuticle picking could be a stim resulting from feelings of stress or anxiety for one client. In this instance, the clinician may center clinical focus on the underlying stress or anxiety. For another client, cheek biting could be a covert form of stimming related to camouflaging (masking). In this instance, the clinician should attend to the impact of camouflaging in general for the client. Yet another client may have struggled with trichotillomania for years, sometimes for hours per day, resulting in bald patches on their scalp. For this client, BFRBs may be a larger focus of treatment. Together, clinicians can work with individuals to identify if the BFRBs themselves are a source of distress outside of the perceptions or reactions of others. If they are a source of distress for the client, they can work together to identify alternative stims, such as using stim toys made specifically for BFRBs. Holistically, clinicians should never pathologize stimming in a general sense and should avoid overpathologizing the presence of BFRBs, especially when they are not a source of significant stress.

Trauma- and Stressor-Related Disorders

Autistic people have higher rates of PTSD and trauma symptomatology, as well as higher levels of adverse childhood experiences (ACEs) compared to allistic individuals (Hartley et al., 2024; Rumball et al., 2021). Autistic individuals are also more likely to be exposed to repeated trauma than allistics, with physical and sexual assault being the most commonly reported traumatic experiences in one study (Rumball et al., 2021). In turn, repeated trauma exposure is associated with greater PTSD symptoms among autistics, with no such relationship found for allistics (Rumball et al., 2021). Interpersonal traumas, like peer victimization, occur more frequently among this population (Libster et al., 2022). Likewise, these interpersonal traumas (including peer victimization, social ostracization, verbal abuse, etc.) are related to increased posttraumatic stress symptoms among autistic, but not allistic adults (Haruvi-Lamdan et al., 2024). Among autistic adults, interpersonal traumas are also positively related to dissociative symptoms (Reuben et al., 2021). Importantly, exposure to Applied Behavior Analysis (or ABA) is also associated with posttraumatic stress symptoms, meaning that clients may have experienced trauma through their past therapeutic experiences (Kupferstein, 2018). With all of this in mind, clinicians should become familiar with how complex trauma, rather than the more narrowed view of trauma within the DSM, can impact client experiences.

Experiencing prolonged stress in which a client's autistic needs are not met can result in Autistic burnout. Autistic burnout is an autism-specific mental health condition associated with severe levels of exhaustion (Arnold et al., 2023). Autistic individuals who experience a non-affirming social environment may mask their autistic traits in order to try to assimilate, which takes a toll on mental health. Masking, non-affirming environments, a lack of support from others, and exceeded demands on the individual together can lead to burnout (Raymaker et al., 2020). Autistic burnout is associated with exhaustion, autistic traits becoming more noticeable, increases in executive functioning concerns, and withdrawing from social environments (Arnold et al., 2023). It is especially important that clinicians are able to distinguish burnout from other conditions, like depression. In depression, behavioral activation is often utilized to increase internal motivation. Autistic burnout is a result of autistic needs consistently being unmet and therefore requires extensive rest and recuperation, alongside finding new strategies or avenues for meeting said needs.

Disordered Eating

Among autistic youth, the prevalence of atypical eating behaviors has been estimated at 70.4 percent (Mayes & Zickgraf, 2019). These eating differences can include a preference for a more narrowed, specific range of foods (sometimes referred to by individuals as "safe foods"), sensory concerns related to food textures, and/or a strong preference for certain brands of foods (Mayes & Zickgraf, 2019). To be clear, these "atypical" preferences are not necessarily an area of concern for autistic clients but may instead reflect a sense of safety and comfort found in eating foods with a high level of sameness compared to allistic eating preferences.

At the same time, eating preferences can emerge as disordered eating at the level of eating disorders among autistic individuals. For individuals with higher levels of disordered eating, Avoidant/Restrictive Food Intake Disorder (ARFID) may be an area of concern (Yule et al., 2021). ARFID is an eating disorder marked by restrictive patterns of eating to the extent that the individual does not meet their nutritional needs (APA, 2022). With the release of the DSM-5, this diagnosis was expanded from a childhood disorder to being able to be diagnosed in a client of any age (Yule et al., 2021). Estimates place 21 percent of autistic individuals at high risk for ARFID (Koomar et al., 2021). Autistic children with ARFID have higher sensory processing concerns than autistic children without ARFID (Kinter et al., 2024). Similarly, oral sensory processing concerns are predictive of ARFID among this population (Kinter et al., 2023). Together, these findings indicate the role that sensory processing concerns play in the development of ARFID among autistic clients.

ARFID is highlighted as a specific concern for the purposes of this work given the high co-occurrence of these diagnoses. However, clinicians should also be cognizant of the prevalence of eating-related concerns among this population in general. For instance, pica, or eating nonfood substances, was estimated at 11.8 percent of autistic children (Mayes & Zickgraf, 2019). There is also a high occurrence of autistic traits among those diagnosed with Anorexia Nervosa (Brown et al., 2024; Westwood & Tchanturia, 2017). Among autistic women, Anorexia Nervosa was the most common previous eating disorder diagnosis reported (Brown et al., 2024). Autistic traits are predictive of disordered eating risk, while the presence of an autism diagnosis is associated with a reduction in disordered eating risk, suggesting that receiving an autism diagnosis is a potential protective factor in this area (Brown et al., 2024). Despite this, among this sample of autistic women, most received a diagnosis of their eating disorder before receiving an autism diagnosis—with a delay of twelve years on average before formal autism diagnosis. (Brown et al., 2024). While outside the scope of the present work, it should also be acknowledged that autistic persons experience high levels of gastrointestinal concerns (Holingue et al., 2018). With the presence of any high level of eating concern, clinicians should work to identify registered dietitians with specific knowledge of autism whenever possible to best collaborate client care.

Addiction

The intersection of autism and addiction is a growing area of concern within both the fields of mental health and neuroscience. Former clinical guidance downplayed the significance of substance use disorders (SUDs) in autism, claiming that it was rare. Some researchers suggested that it was the presence of ADHD in co-occurring ADHD/ASD that could increase the risk of SUDs in neurodivergent individuals (Palmqvist, Edman, Bölte,

2012). However, more modern research has expounded on the complex relationship between autism and substance use, finding that autistic people—*without* co-occurring ADHD or intellectual disability—are two to six times more likely to develop a substance use-related problem compared to the general population (Butwicka et al., 2017; Lundström et al., 2011), a reality that many of our clinical colleagues have recognized in their work with autistic adults. Rates of addiction in autistic adults vary drastically based on the operationalized definitions of both "autistic" and "addiction" (from 0.7% to 36%; Arnevik & Helvershou, 2016), a methodological problem that lends confusion to clinicians regarding the population prevalence of addiction in autistic people. This is another instance in which we recommend clinicians re-direct focus toward the needs of individual clients.

While the prevalence of addiction or substance use-related problems is debated, the underlying mechanisms for the increased prevalence have been hypothesized. The hypothesis we find most compelling based on our clinical experiences centers on the intersection of autistic sensory processing needs and the numbing effects of substances (van den Boogert et al., 2024). These researchers found that sensory processing differences in autistic adults were correlated with increased alcohol use and increased prevalence of binge drinking. While the nature of the research design prohibits causal conclusions, we do find the results compelling given our clinical experiences—which include many instances of autistic adults regularly using depressant drugs (alcohol, benzodiazepines) as a means of sensory regulation.

In our discussion of the etiology of addiction in autistic people, we'd be remiss to not mention the social realities of living as an autistic person and the ways in which the presence of alcohol can act as the "Great Social Equalizer." I (Chris) once had an adult autistic client who exclusively got drunk in social situations with unfamiliar people. During our work together, we discovered that their drunkenness in those situations was a way to protect them from the embarrassment of being themselves in the presence of potentially unsupportive people who may not understand their autistic ways of being. By being drunk, they reduced themselves to a stereotype more consumable by their allistic peers—a drunk person. Any subsequent embarrassment could be attached to their unstable persona of their intoxicated self rather than their stable identity as an autistic person.

These social realities influencing autistic drug use have been reaffirmed in the literature (Bowri et al., 2021).

Borderline Personality Disorder

Personality disorders are among the most frequently perceived misdiagnoses among autistic individuals, with autistic women appearing to be disproportionately impacted in this area (Kentrou et al., 2024). On the surface, there are external similarities between these clinical presentations, including the potential for emotional dysregulation, a history of interpersonal concerns or trauma, and a higher likelihood of suicidality and NSSI (McQuaid et al., 2024). Alongside this, as discussed previously, autistic individuals are evaluated more negatively than non-autistic individuals based on brief interactions, with these impressions being more negative among those with higher levels of autism knowledge only when an autism diagnosis is specifically disclosed (Sasson et al., 2017). This reality paired with the fact that clinicians sometimes utilize "clinical instinct" and a "gut feeling" when identifying Borderline Personality Disorder (Wlodarczyk et al., 2018, p. 6), alongside biases in viewing autism as a male disorder (Brickhill et al., 2023), clinicians may be more likely to ascribe similar clinical presentations among women to BPD instead of autism. However, this is an emerging area within the literature, and further research is needed to clarify the complexities in this area.

Women who were previously diagnosed with BPD before receiving an autism diagnosis indicated that the BPD label alone did not fully fit their experiences and led to bias from practitioners, alongside barriers to accessing care (Powell et al., 2024). Among those participants who felt alignment with both diagnoses, they described that the dual diagnoses allowed them to more fully understand their experiences and find adequate support (Powell et al., 2024). These findings provide nuance, in that BPD can both be a misdiagnosis, as well as an avenue for self-understanding among this population. Further research is needed to clarify the co-occurrence of these diagnoses, as well as to identify adequate interventions and supports.

∞

A Case Study in Complex Differential Diagnosis

Bethany (she/her) is a forty-two-year-old, White, cisgender, pansexual woman from a rural Midwestern town. She appeared for a psychological diagnostic evaluation due to conflicting past diagnoses which made treatment planning difficult for her current individual therapist. I (Chris) saw this client for psychological differential diagnosis. The client had historical diagnoses of Bipolar I Disorder, Intermittent Explosive Disorder, Social Anxiety Disorder (Social Phobia), Borderline Personality Disorder, and Major Depressive Disorder. The client left my care with one diagnostic label: Autism Spectrum Disorder. After our comprehensive evaluation and testing, each of the client's differences was better explained by unaccommodated, unsupported autism. Their Intermittent Explosive Disorder was diagnosed due to "temper tantrums" (read: autistic meltdowns). Their Bipolar I diagnosis mostly hinged on excessive irritability caused by unmet sensory needs (it was also a probable misdiagnosis; there was no evidence they ever experienced mania). Their Major Depressive Disorder symptoms (fatigue, difficulty concentrating, anhedonia) matched better with autistic burnout (which they scored high on). Their Borderline Personality Disorder was diagnosed based on emotional regulation difficulties, feelings of shame, and categorical thinking (all common in autistic people). After conducting a neuro-affirming and trauma-informed evaluation, it was clinically clear that Bethany was one of the many autistic women who were misdiagnosed throughout life with anything but autism. It only took one autism-informed clinician to see this in Bethany. With this text, we hope to help you be that clinician for a client one day.

Conclusion

In summary, autistic individuals are more likely to experience a variety of co-occurring conditions. Importantly, autistic individuals also have higher prevalence rates of other diagnostic categories this guide did not touch upon, including but not limited to: other personality disorders and schizophrenia spectrum disorders (Lugo-Marín et al., 2019). In a sample of late-diagnosed adults, prior to receiving an autism diagnosis, most had previous contact with mental health services, with 66.5 percent being previously diagnosed with something other than ASD (Fusar-Poli et al., 2022). In fact, individuals diagnosed in adulthood were significantly more likely to have a previous psychiatric diagnosis than those diagnosed in childhood (Jadav & Bal, 2022). Because of this, clinicians should consider autism as a possibility at the onset of treatment—not as a last resort—when working with clients who are demonstrating characteristics of the diagnostic labels discussed in this section. Similarly, clinicians should not mistake the presence of any of these conditions as a rule-out for autism. A failure to consider autism and discuss such considerations with clients perpetuates stigma against autism through reinforcing it as something unapproachable—something that even professionals cannot speak about openly without judgment. Clinicians must remain alert to the high prevalence of anti-autistic bias present within the field and within the broader literature when working to understand their autistic clients. Most importantly, clinicians must focus on listening to their autistic client's internal experiences. In doing so, they can be a part of healing systemic harms to autistic clients on an interpersonal basis.

Critical Thinking Questions

1. What are some potential consequences of misdiagnosis on the well-being and treatment outcomes of autistic clients? What do you think may contribute to the high level of misdiagnosis among autistic clients?
2. How might clinicians adapt common therapeutic approaches to better meet the needs of autistic clients with co-occurring conditions? What unique strategies could be incorporated to ensure these interventions are affirming and responsive to autistic perspectives?
3. How may treatment of OCD look different between an autistic and allistic client?

5

Intervention Approaches

Learning Outcomes

1. Recognize autism as a natural variation in the human genome and explore how this perspective influences intervention.
2. Understand the strengths and challenges of autistic communication styles.
3. Identify common interventions in autistic care, including trauma-informed approaches.
4. Develop an understanding of the importance of interdisciplinary care.
5. Critically interrogate the utility of traditional autism "treatment" and intervention.

For clarity on our position, discussing "treatment" and "intervention" for ASD paints us firmly into a biomedical corner (see Chapter 1 for comparison between different models of understanding autism). That is, to "treat" insinuates an ailment—this is controversial among many in the autism community. Many autistic people see their autism not as an overarching ailment but as a natural variation in the human genome with concomitant unique strengths. From this vantage, autistic ways of being (called "symptoms" in the biomedical model) are inherently worthy ways of being which society is called to support, value, and celebrate.

Social Communication and Awareness Support

Autistic communication styles, while diverse and multifaceted, bring about a wealth of strengths that enrich interpersonal interactions and contribute unique perspectives to our society. In this section, we attempt to strike a balance between acknowledging existing strengths of autistic communication and highlighting potential social communication challenges that are among some of the prominent diagnostic features of autism spectrum disorder. For the latter, we offer evidence-based suggestions for support and intervention.

Many autistic people communicate in a straightforward, direct manner that values honesty and clarity over tact. While logical and sensical, a direct communication style may be upsetting to people who do not share the same communication style. Ironically, the directness and transparency that is often part and parcel of autistic communication may lead to misunderstandings and confusion among allistic individuals who have internalized ambiguous communication styles. Other autistic individuals need higher levels of support in developing communication, described in further depth in Chapter 3. While the burden of adapting communication should not fall squarely on the shoulders of autistic people, there can be merit to learning different communication styles in ways that do not demonize or minimize preferred or natural communication. Clinicians, especially neurotypical and allistic clinicians, working with autistic clients may want to carefully approach social communication interventions so as to not imply that the communication styles of autistic clients are innately wrong, bad, or dysfunctional, as such forms of social skills training can be experienced as stigmatizing by autistic individuals (Hull et al., 2024). Instead, autistic individuals value social skills support that is personalized, depathologizing, and interactive (Hull et al., 2024).

Exploring Camouflaging of Autistic Traits

Some autistic clients utilize masking, or camouflaging, as a social strategy to facilitate communication with allistic individuals (Cook et al., 2021;

Hull et al., 2017; Livingston et al., 2019). Camouflaging includes both an outward suppression of external autistic traits (such as decreasing stimming behaviors or minimizing an autistic communication style) and increasing communication strategies to appear more outwardly neurotypical (like intentionally mirroring the body language and eye contact of one's conversation partner or preparing for conversations through scripting them ahead of time). For autistic individuals, this process can be cognitively taxing and thus, perhaps unsurprisingly, is associated with negative mental health outcomes (Hull et al., 2021).

Beneath the external surface, masking can distance autistic individuals from their internal sense of self (Livingston et al., 2019). Given the focus of masking on facilitating interactions with others, autistic clients can over time become less attuned to their own internal feelings, desires, and needs. Masking can be conscious or unconscious, meaning that clients may not be aware of all of the ways in which they are engaging in masking, let alone what the internal impacts may be. Sessions may focus on processing the ways in which masking has been (and may remain) a protective strategy for clients. Experiencing autism-related stigma is predictive of masking, and masking is utilized as a strategy to protect against peer victimization (Cage & Troxell-Whitman, 2019; Perry et al., 2022).

Because of this connection, as clients explore the construct of masking within session, they may also, in turn, explore the emotional experiences the process of masking is linked to. As a client begins to "unmask" in more environments, they may uncover suppressed emotions related to past interpersonal experiences or traumas. For instance, one client I (Audrey) worked with began the process of consciously unmasking in the majority of their social environments. In turn, the client began experiencing a significant level of free-floating, physical anxiety that they could not place. After further exploration, they discovered that they were experiencing similar anxious distress to what they experienced during a traumatic time period in their life in which minimizing their feelings and needs was protective. The therapeutic alliance may be utilized as an avenue for exploring the emotional undercurrent of the process of unmasking in the moment. Inherent to this process is valuing the client for their authentic self, as a contrast to internalization of anti-autistic bias that may manifest as shame or self-loathing.

Mindfulness and Relaxation

Mindfulness is a practice rooted in Eastern philosophy and spiritual practice, and it has found its way into Western therapeutic interventions. Summarized simply, mindfulness interventions focus on bringing one's attention to the present moment in a non-judgmental way. Mindfulness has shown promise in various therapeutic domains, including enhancing social communication and awareness in autistic individuals. Social Cognition Training (SCT) complements mindfulness by addressing how individuals process, store, and apply information about others in social situations. For autistic clients, a combination of mindfulness practices and SCT may offer a holistic approach to enhancing perspective-taking, emotional regulation, and improving social cue attentional awareness (de Bruin et al., 2015).

Mindfulness practice has been incorporated into a variety of somatic approaches to autism intervention. Yoga, combining physical postures with breath control and meditation exercises, has been explored as a therapeutic modality for autism (Koenig et al., 2012). Regular yoga practice can lead to better motor skills, improved self-awareness, and reduced anxiety, which can indirectly support social interactions. Progressive muscle relaxation, another exercise that combines somatic connection and mindfulness, has been shown to help autistic individuals become more aware of physical sensations and can be an effective tool in managing anxiety or agitation (Conner & White, 2018). Lastly, biofeedback, a technique that teaches individuals to control physiological functions, has been shown to lead to improvements in emotional and physiological regulation in autistic people during social interactions (Kouijzer et al., 2009).

Creativity can be utilized in adapting existing mindfulness interventions to best meet the needs of individual autistic clients. If an autistic client struggles with sitting still, a quiet meditation may not suit said client's needs. Instead, that client may identify ways to mindfully self-soothe with sensory activities, like feeling the sensation of their hand in a bag of rice. Or, a visual timer may give this client an external, grounding focus while engaging in a breathing exercise. An autistic client who struggles with figurative language may not connect with a progressive muscle relaxation video that speaks about imagining streams of light entering their tense muscle groups but may better appreciate a video that explains in specific detail how to go about the process of tensing and relaxing their muscles. Favorite topics or interests can also be incorporated. For instance, a clinician specifically labeling a client's enjoyment of sorting or organizing their collection of diecast cars as a mindful activity could help a client to affirm a tool they already have in their toolkit. Listening to clients when they explain what does not work for them about certain approaches can lead to collaborative solutions that clients can actually use effectively.

∞

Interoception refers to the ability to perceive and understand internal bodily cues and sensations such as hunger, thirst, heart rate, and emotions. Many autistic individuals experience differences in interoception, which can impact their ability to recognize internal signals (e.g., this autistic TikTok creator often discusses her difficulties with recognizing thirst: https://www.tiktok.com/@soundoftheforest?lang=en). Mindfulness practices, while often clinically implemented to reduce anticipatory or future-oriented anxiety through techniques that privilege the present moment, can also be used to assist autistic client's interoceptive abilities. For example, body scans can be used to help autistic people tune in to their current bodily needs! (Note: Body scans can be distressing for clients who have a history of physical trauma and should be incorporated with caution toward the client's experiences with said intervention).

Emotions and Alexithymia

In contrast to stereotypes of autistic individuals as emotionless or robotic, autistic persons experience complex internal emotional states that are often misunderstood by neurotypical people (Dallman, 2024). Autistic adults appear to experience higher levels of mixed emotional states, or both positively valenced and negatively valenced emotions at once (Costache et al., 2024). Some research indicates that autistic clients experience higher levels of difficult emotions (sadness and anxiety) as well as lower levels of positive emotions (including calm, joy, and interest) (Costache et al.,

2024). Alongside providing autistic clients with avenues for coping with difficult emotions, therapy can focus on helping clients to become more attuned to their experiences of autistic joy. Stimming behaviors help clients to regulate and express emotional states (Charlton et al., 2021; Kapp et al., 2019). Stimming also provides a means for expressing or evoking happiness or peacefulness (Petty & Ellis, 2024). Through external, social pressures, autistic clients can become distanced from their form of emotional expression and regulation. Therefore, identifying avenues for utilizing sensory experience or bodily movements can increase emotional attunement.

With these complex emotions, about half of autistic individuals struggle with alexithymia, or a difficulty identifying and communicating about said emotions (Kinnaird et al., 2019). Alexithymia is related to interoceptive concerns among autistic people, or a difficulty identifying internal physical signals or cues, and lower levels of emotional control or regulation (Bird & Cook, 2013; Ben Hassen et al., 2023; Costache et al., 2024). Pragmatically, if a client has difficulty identifying internal emotional signals in small day-to-day moments, they are more likely to experience a buildup of emotions that can be experienced as distressing (e.g., panic attacks, explosive anger, meltdowns, and shutdowns), thus reinforcing patterns of emotional avoidance that may accompany emotional identification concerns. Within sessions, alexithymia can also outwardly appear as intellectualization of emotions as clients work to understand their internal experiences

Alongside aiding the client in distress tolerance for bigger emotional moments, therapeutic interventions can be utilized to help clients attune to their internal emotional experiences, as well as communicate about said experiences to their provider. Dr. Neff has designed a workbook specifically oriented toward aiding neurodivergent clients with their experiences of alexithymia (n.d.). Included in this workbook are a multitude of suggestions to help clients connect to their emotions, including utilizing tools like emotion wheels, emotional thermometers, the matrix of emotions, or by using tools already available to clients, like music. Autistic clients can utilize their pattern recognition abilities toward beginning to recognize patterns of physical emotional signals as they occur in order to move toward processing emotions in the moment. Additionally, clients can be encouraged to do emotional check-ins throughout the day when they experience more delayed emotional processing (recognizing emotions following initial emotional experiences)

Through these interventions, we believe that autistic individuals can become more attuned with their emotional needs over time.

Below we have included one visual avenue for thinking about health and well-being among autistic clients: the autistic self-care sunflower. This tool can be used to help clients think about what avenues they have for engaging in self-care, both in relation to their emotional well-being, as well as related to other aspects of autistic wellness. A printable version of this resource, which autistic clients can fill in themselves in session, is located Appendix D.

Safety Planning with Autistic Clients

As discussed in Chapter 4, autistic individuals disproportionately experience suicidal ideation and non-suicidal self-injury (NSSI) as compared to allistic individuals. One avenue for supporting autistic clients with these experiences is the creation of a safety plan with resources and coping skills which they can utilize during times of crisis. The creation of safety plans can at times be a uniform procedure by providers or agencies. However, autistic individuals have expressed the need for safety planning to be a flexible, dynamic process (Goodwin et al., 2024). For example, some autistic individuals may benefit from receiving a copy of the safety plan to review prior to their first session or appointment, while others may need more than one session in order to complete their plan (Goodwin et al., 2024). This may at times be an additional navigation for providers working with autistic clients, as autistic clients experiencing high levels of emotional distress may not be able to fully engage in the creation of a safety plan until they are in a more emotionally regulated state (Goodwin et al., 2024).

Some individuals benefit from visual supports, such as visuals of coping skills, while creating the plan or to be given examples of potential coping skills they can utilize in their plan by their provider, rather than being expected to think of ideas on their own (Goodwin et al., 2024). Others may prefer to have a supportive person in their life to collaborate with them on the safety planning process (Goodwin et al., 2024). Checking in with each autistic client about the formatting of their safety plan (including

Figure 5.1 The Autistic Self-Care Sunflower allows clients to identify areas of self-care in a variety of areas related to autistic well-being.

whether they prefer a digital copy or a paper copy, the font and visual structure of their plan, the language utilized in the plan, etc.) can help to ensure that any plan created can be utilized effectively by the client (Goodwin et al., 2024).

Adapted safety plans specifically for neurodivergent clients are slowly becoming more readily available. For instance, The Neurodivergent Friendly Workbook of DBT Skills has a mapping tool specifically for experiences of autistic meltdowns (Wise, 2022). Some autistic individuals engage in NSSI during meltdowns, such as head banging, self-hitting, scratching, or cutting (Lewis et al., 2023). The creation of a safety plan can help clients to have a reminder of resources or coping tools for such experiences in order to reduce potential harm. The creation of a safety plan can also help autistic clients with interoceptive concerns to identify warning signs that they may be approaching a dysregulated state. This is one intervention that can help autistic individuals to value their internal emotional experiences. Autistic clients can also give meltdown information sheets to caregivers, roommates, or close loved ones that inform others on how they should respond to or support the client while they are experiencing a meltdown (Wise, 2022). For instance, some autistic clients may need to communicate through alternative methods rather than speaking verbally during moments of high emotional intensity. Having a plan in place can ensure that loved ones know how to support an autistic individual effectively.

Safety planning for meltdowns can also include the creation of a self-care toolkit with easily accessible supports. For instance, if a client engages in NSSI related to a high need for sensory input during meltdowns or shutdowns, a toolkit may include other avenues for receiving intense sensory input, like popsicle sticks the client can break or paper they can tear. If a client experiences dissociative symptoms during meltdowns or shutdowns, a toolkit may include grounding tools like fidget objects, sour candy, or scented markers. Through true collaboration between provider and client, safety plans can be a helpful tool for clients through difficult emotional experiences.

∞

Case Studies in Safety Planning

Matthew is a ninteen-year-old autistic man who lives with a neurodivergent roommate. He is seeking therapy to focus on emotional regulation. He describes having "meltdowns," during which he experiences overwhelming emotions and cannot suppress his need to externalize his internal pain through sobbing or yelling. The shame he feels surrounding times his meltdowns have scared people in his life compounds his difficulties in regulating his emotions during these moments. Since his new roommate is supportive, Matthew creates a meltdown information sheet to share with him. This tool allows him to explain his experiences with meltdowns to his roommate, which, in turn, allows Matthew to feel less ashamed about his experiences. Over time, as Matthew's ability to regulate emotions and his level of self-compassion increase, his experiences with meltdowns become less frequent.

Leo is a twenty-year-old, autistic nonbinary person seeking therapy to increase emotional awareness. They describe periods of "shut-downs" during which they experience passive suicidal thoughts. During these episodes, Leo can feel disconnected from their body and the world around them. They utilize non-suicidal self-injury through cutting in order to feel more connected to the present moment. In session, they create a safety plan which includes reducing access to the knife they use to engage in NSSI. They create a toolkit to carry in their bag with other grounding tools they can utilize for their dissociative experiences. Through interventions focused on decreasing alexithymia, Leo becomes more attuned to warning signs of shutdowns, and their experiences with shutdowns decrease.

Emily is a twenty-year-old graduate student seeking therapy for what she initially describes as "panic attacks" related to social anxiety. She explains that when she gets back to her house after tiring social events, she has marked periods of uncontrollable anger, during which she may hit her head on the floor repeatedly. Through further exploration of her experiences in session, Emily is found to more likely be undiagnosed autistic than socially anxious. Through planning with her therapist, she works to create a place of safety in her room with pillows she can bury her head into if she has overwhelming emotions. Making a safety plan helps her to recognize that her masking behaviors contribute to her not recognizing her internal signals of discomfort during social events because she is so focused on how others perceive her, instead of her internal needs. As Emily finds places in life she can openly be herself, her emotions become more regulated.

Trauma-Informed Care with Autistic Clients

As discussed in Chapter 5, autistic persons have elevated rates of trauma-related symptomatology as compared to allistic individuals (Rumball et al., 2021). Because of this, and in alignment with broader principles of trauma-informed care, regular screening for trauma-related symptoms should be implemented in practice with autistic clients (Butler et al., 2011). Within the clinical practice of the authors, the intersection between autistic experience and trauma can at times appear largely ubiquitous. Fulton and colleagues (2020) have denoted the idea of "sensory trauma" among autistic persons, in which the unavoidable nature of discomforting sensory experiences may differentially impact daily anxiety, noting that autistic experiences with trauma may intersect with autistic experience in an allistic world. Alongside this, some autistic individuals have experienced trauma within therapy settings specifically (Darazsdi & Bialka, 2023).

For autistic clients with a history of feeling misunderstood, misconstrued, minimized, and mistreated—or misdiagnosed—therapy can offer an avenue for relational healing. This can be achieved through taking time and care to establish safety within the therapy setting and within the therapeutic alliance, through acknowledging power dynamics within the setting, and through giving clients agency in establishing what does and does not work for them in treatment. When autistic clients engage in behaviors or experience difficulties that allistic practitioners have difficulty empathizing with, there may be a tendency for such practitioners to retreat to more surface-level techniques and interventions as an avenue of support. We believe that deeper relational connections with clients are an important aspect of healing from past relational traumas and should be prioritized.

Peer Support and Group Therapy

One primary neuro-affirming intervention that is being increasingly recognized as a valuable component in mental health work with autistic individuals is peer support. Engaging with peers who have shared similar lived experiences offers autistic people a sense of validation and understanding that is hard to replicate in other settings. Peer support interactions can significantly reduce feelings of isolation, foster a sense of community, and enhance overall well-being (Mazurek, 2014). Organizations have recognized the importance of peer support programs, implementing them in a variety of settings. For example, the American Psychological Association houses the Disability Mentoring Program, which pairs disabled psychology students (including autistic students) with professional mentors, and The University of Montana at Missoula houses the Mentoring, Organization and Social Support for Autism Inclusion on Campus (MOSSAIC) Program. Within MOSSAIC, autistic mentees receive support from mentors on social interactions, executive functioning, and academics (Locke et al., 2024). Both mentors and mentees appreciated the contributions of an autistic self-advocate to the program, indicating the importance of autistic involvement in similar programs (Locke et al., 2024).

Within clinical settings, group therapy can be an avenue toward peer support. Group therapy can aid autistic clients toward building a positive autistic identity, alongside learning pragmatic coping skills from others with shared experiences (Crane et al., 2021). Autistic individuals have expressed a preference for group therapy to be designed or implemented by autistic facilitators when possible (Crane et al., 2020; Hull et al., 2024). This may in part, be related to the ability of autistic mental health professionals to connect with autistic clients (Dabbs et al., 2024). When such facilitation is not possible, there are still avenues for empowering autistic individuals within group therapy settings. For instance, Rankin and colleagues (2024) incorporated a self-advocacy module into their group therapy approach for autistic adults that allowed clients to design and present to a group of healthcare professionals on topics related to best serving autistic clients. When creating a group, it is important to continually involve the clients being served in order to continually shift the group to meet their needs.

In group therapy, autistic clients can appreciate a certain amount of structure in order to understand the rules of the group setting and know what to expect. For instance, process-oriented questions for group discussions may be provided to clients ahead of the group meeting so that they have time to consider their thoughts and prepare responses, rather than feeling put on the spot. Even with more structure, some autistic clients may prefer to take on a listening role more than they contribute. More traditional schools of group therapy may pathologize a client who has a preference for engaging in group settings quietly, but this may be a way in which some clients best take in information. Other clients may be highly engaged and talkative within group settings, speaking more than other group members. Clear communication can be utilized with all group members if unevenness in time spent on one member is negatively impacting other members. At the same time, group therapy with autistic clients may naturally appear less li allistic communication within group settings, which may require adjustment for an allistic facilitator to align with as an outsider.

Collaborative and Interdisciplinary Care

From the vast array of services and types of care written about in this guide, to the occupational diversity of the authors, it may be no surprise that holistic and collaborative care can be instrumental to the wellness of autistic individuals. Given the multifaceted nature of autism—social, cognitive, communicative, behavioral—interventions almost necessitate an interdisciplinary approach that tailors evolving needs across the lifespan. A "cookie-cutter" approach to autism care does not suffice because, as autistic professor of special education and autism advocate Dr. Stephen Shore remarked, "if you've met one person with autism, you've met one person with autism" (Lime Network, n.d.).

The above quote highlights one of the nuances of autism—the variability of differences. Autism (and autism spectrum disorder) has a vast and heterogeneous presentation. While one individual may have heightened sensory processing needs or sensitivities, another might primarily face social communication challenges. Given the diversity of presentations in autism, maintaining a holistic understanding through the shared expertise of a diverse care team can be vital to the success of autistic people.

Applied Behavioral Analysis

ABA has long been celebrated as the "gold standard" for "treating" symptoms of autism. ABA uses principles of behaviorism (rewards, conditioning, punishment, etc.) to modify target behaviors. Autistic self-advocates have for years expressed concerns surrounding ABA, leading to discord between self-advocates and institutional powers within the field. While fully addressing the nuances of this area is outside the scope of the present work, we align ourselves with those who view the conceptual roots of ABA as non-affirming toward autistic experiences.

We have significant concerns with the foundations and principles of this discipline, namely we care first and foremost about the internal experiences of autistic individuals. In contrast, ABA research has largely centered on limited behavioral outcome measures as indicators of success—within reductions of autistic traits delineating a "successful" outcome. Furthermore, a review of behavioral research in this area indicated the majority of studies (84%) were conducted by authors with conflicts of interest that only 2 percent adequately disclosed (Bottema-Beutel & Crowley, 2021). In addition, a review in this area draws into question the efficacy of this modality compared to other approaches, noting alongside this conclusion the regularity of risk for bias in ABA outcome studies (Rodgers et al., 2020).

Limited research that does center on the lived experiences of autistic individuals indicates that ABA is associated with trauma for autistic clients (Anderson et al., 2023; Kuperferstein, 2018; McGuill & Robinson, 2020). One autistic individual who previously experienced ABA stated that, "The idea that being indistinguishable is something to be looked for, that it's positive, is just plain wrong" (Anderson, 2022, p. 744). While interventions and methods can differ by practitioner, a 2008 study of ABA experts found that 62.5 percent approved of overcorrection (a form of punishment), 72.5 percent of seclusion timeout, 43.1 percent of physical punishment, 34.6 percent of sensory punishment, and 26.9 percent of contingent electric shock (Brown et al., 2008).

While incremental reforms in the field are undoubtedly improvements, such incrementalism ultimately has not yet addressed systemic harms. Recent movements within ABA have demonstrated a desire to acknowledge harms within the field and to listen to the lived experiences of autistic people (Mathu et al., 2024). This call includes a desire to meet the needs of autistic ABA trainees and clinicians. We appreciate the growing movement among ABA providers who acknowledge from their viewpoint toward autistic self-advocacy that "How we respond to the criticisms levied against our field will define us as much, if not more, than the criticisms themselves," rooted in the perspective that "We must believe them" (Mathu et al., 2024, p. Conclusion section para. 1 & 2). Given the complexities in this area, we recommend the Autism Self Advocacy Network's comprehensive overview if you are interested in learning about this area in more depth: https://autisticadvocacy.org/wp-content/uploads/2021/12/ACWP-Ethics-of-Intervention.pdf.

Critical Thinking Questions

1. How could you adapt the mindfulness exercises you typically utilize with clients for those with high levels of executive functioning concerns?
2. What challenges may there be in working with a client with high levels of alexithymia?
3. What are your initial reactions to the complicated history of ABA? What could neuro-affirming ABA look like (if you believe that to be possible)?

6

Supporting Autistic Clients in Everyday Life

Learning Outcomes

1. Explore strategies for creating sensory friendly environments for autistic clients.
2. Understand the importance of Individualized Education Plans in tailoring education to meet specific needs.
3. Explore the challenges that autistic students face during life transitions.
4. Elaborate on the importance of employment and healthcare supports for autistic clients.

Educational Support

Autistic students often face a unique set of challenges in educational settings, ranging from sensory sensitivities to social interaction difficulties and differences in executive function (Ashburner et al., 2010). For example, the bright fluorescent lighting in a classroom and the ambient noise may be overwhelming to an autistic student due to heightened sensory sensitivities. Additionally, group work or unstructured social time can pose challenges due to potential mismatches in communication styles or differences in social communication.

To address these challenges, many educational institutions, in collaboration with students and caregivers, may implement Individualized Education Plans (IEPs). IEPs provide a tailored approach to teaching, learning, and assessment, ensuring that the student's needs are met (Whitaker, 2007). Additionally, the provision of safe, quiet areas in schools has been recognized as a valuable resource. These quiet areas act as a refuge where autistic students can retreat if they feel overwhelmed, providing them a moment of reprieve and a chance to recenter themselves (see Chapter 6 for mindfulness-based suggestions and interventions).

Additionally, educators have discussed the benefits of sensory supports in the class. The implementation of sensory tools, such as "fidget toys" (also called "focus tools"), and allowing breaks for sensory management, may lead to better task focus and active participation in the classroom (Whitaker, 2007). Some researchers have recognized the utility of sensory focus tools and breaks for people with both autism and ADHD, which tend to co-occur at high rates (see Chapter 5; Biel, 2017). Ear protection (headphones, noise-reducing earplugs, etc.) has likewise been recognized as an avenue for increasing the comfort of autistic students with ambient classroom noise (Kulawiak, 2021). Finally, the implementation of peer mentoring has been transformative for many autistic people (discussed more in-depth in Chapter 6; Whitaker, 2007). By pairing autistic students with other autistic students or understanding peers, schools can foster environments of inclusivity, understanding, and mutual growth.

Life transitions can be especially challenging for autistic individuals. As autistic students reach high school, transition planning can be incorporated into IEPs in order to aid students as they move into the next chapter of their lives following the completion of secondary education (Szidon et al., 2015). Transition planning begins by identifying, with the autistic student, goals for living, employment, and education following high school (Szidon et al., 2015). Next, these goals can be matched with specific, measurable IEP goals in order to prepare students to develop the skills needed to meet their desired outcomes. These goals can be updated each year as the student moves closer to graduation. As discussed in the following section, the world of employment can be complicated for autistic individuals, so additional support in school settings can help to facilitate successful transitions.

Employment Support

The spiky profile of each autistic person mirrors a similar diversity in career trajectories and coinciding support needs among the autistic community. Some autistic individuals hold 9–5 office jobs, others participate in adult day habilitation programs, while others have no occupation and receive government disability benefits. Anthropological analysis suggests a necessary balancing act for disability justice in this area: between encouraging independence in work through supportive avenues and through avoiding equating economic earning potential with meaning-making in life (Grinker, 2020). In a similar avenue, clinicians may support an autistic client in gaining fulfilling employment if that is within their treatment goals, while also advocating for broader social changes for disabled persons of all occupational paths.

In a national US workplace report of autistic individuals, researchers found that autistic employment post-high school was only 42 percent, over afivefold increase over the general disabled unemployment rate in the United States (Roux et al., 2015; US Bureau of Labor Statistics, 2025). These numbers have also been corroborated by other Western countries. The United Kingdom Office for National Statistics has reported that autistic people were among those with the lowest employment rate (21.7%; Putz et al., 2021). These employment rates also differ by other intersectional factors. For instance, one study found that only 37 percent of Black autistic young adults were employed compared to 66 percent of White autistic young adults (Roux et al., 2015, as cited in Malone et al., 2022).

Day Habilitation Programs and Sheltered Workshops

Some autistic individuals may participate in non-traditional work environments like day habilitation programs or sheltered workshops. Day habilitation programming includes focus in a variety of areas, including activities of daily living (ADLs), social recreation, physical activity, self-care, and vocational support (Gerhardt et al., 2014). Individuals who participate in these programs may also reside in supported living environments. Autistic adults may also participate in sheltered workshops (Gerhardt et al., 2014). These are segregated settings for disabled people which in the United States under Section 14(c) of the Fair Labor Standards Act allow for hourly payment below the minimum wage (US Commission on Civil Rights, 2020).

These programs are marked as contentious by disability rights activists, with Schwartz and Moore (2021) explaining that they leave disabled persons in "a lifetime of tedious work at indecent wages—frequently less than a dollar an hour—and rarely lead to meaningful work" (p. 1). These workshops allow for minimal contact with non-disabled employees—in contrast with standards set by the Americans with Disabilities Act (Schwarts & Moore, 2021). Additionally, these programs offer fewer employment protections, including being denied the ability to unionize (US Commission on Civil Rights, 2020). Research also calls into question the viability of sheltered workshops as transitional resources for increasing future employment potential for autistic persons (Cimera et al., 2012). While adults receiving autism-specific services have shared appreciation for increased social avenues with other autistic individuals, they have also expressed desires for participation in larger community activities focused on their areas of interest rather than segregated activities alone (Koffer Miller et al., 2018).

However, the majority of disabled individuals (83–90%) and their family members (95–96%) who submitted comments to an investigation of the subminimum wage by the US Commission on Civil Rights in 2020 advocated for maintaining 14(c) regulations. Disabled persons expressed fears surrounding losing their current employment or making less money without 14(c) protections, as well as enjoying the community provided by their current place of work (U.S. Commission on Civil Rights, 2020). Therefore, it is important that all disabled persons are given informed choice in their employment decisions, including the supportive structures needed for making that choice (Moore & Friedman, 2017).

In recent years, competitive integrated employment (CIE) has been increasingly viewed as a viable employment option for many autistic individuals (Brooke et al., 2018). A recent systematic review of the literature found that CIE allowed for better quality of life, mental health outcomes, autonomy and independence, and earning potential when compared with segregated working environments for adults with intellectual and developmental disabilities (Taylor et al., 2023). Through utilizing vocational rehabilitation services, 87.1 percent of autistic individuals were able to obtain and retain CIE (Brooke et al., 2018). Importantly, 11.5 percent of individuals who remained employed continued to need high or moderate amounts of support (Brooke et al., 2018). In this way, continued reforms should prioritize service options for all levels of support needs, including those for whom CIE is not a viable option.

However, integration into CIE settings can also present added financial complications for disabled persons. Presently in the United States, disabled individuals face a resource limit of $2,000 in order to retain Supplemental Security Income (SSI) (Social Security Administration, 2023). For married individuals, this limit is $3,000, placing a tangible barrier toward marriage equality for this group (Social Security Administration, n.d.). Among autistic individuals participating in service programs in Pennsylvania, 75 percent indicated concerns about losing benefits and resources if their income level increased (Koffer Miller et al., 2017). Practitioners should continue to advocate for legislation that furthers equity, informed choice, and a multitude of options for disabled individuals. A large component in the massive influence of inequitable practices against disabled individuals are social stigmas and misunderstandings.

Stigma and Misperceptions

The stigma and misperceptions born from the Double Empathy Problem have significant repercussions in the adult autistic community, particularly in the realm of employment. While there are a myriad of reasons why autistic adults may be some of the most unemployed or underemployed individuals of any difference category, some of the largest contributors are negative workplace attitudes and lack of understanding regarding autistic people (Black et al., 2020). Service providers (including clinicians) view stigma as less significant barrier to employment than autistic individuals (Black et al., 2020), meaning that clinicians may at times underestimate the level and impact of the stigma that their autistic clients face.

Current national US statistics show that approximately 69 percent of employed autistic adults work in jobs that are not public-facing (e.g., food preparation, building maintenance, office support staff; Roux et al., 2015). While the reality of autistic people in the workforce may be a gravitation (or sociocultural pushing) toward operational employment, this does not preclude autistic individuals from working in interpersonal, public-facing occupations—such as those in the mental health fields. However, due to the aforementioned stigma and stereotypes, autistic individuals desiring public-facing occupations may be systematically gatekept from participating. For instance, autistic mental health professionals experience interpersonal and systemic ableism within their graduate training programs, which negatively impacts their personal wellbeing (Dabbs et al., 2024). Additionally, these stigma-related concerns are influenced by other social identities. Transgender, autistic employees report lower levels of workplace inclusion and authenticity as compared to cisgender, autistic employees (Doyle et al., 2022). Likewise, Black, autistic employees indicate lower levels of workplace support and a higher perceived need to mask their autistic traits compared to White, autistic employees (Doyle et al., 2022).

Navigating the world of employment can be particularly challenging for many autistic adults because of the aforementioned reasons. This is despite the strengths that autistic individuals bring to the workplace, including being more likely to voice concerns related to workplace dysfunction and being less likely to be influenced by others in their decision to voice concerns (Hartman et al., 2023). In this way, autistic individuals may be uniquely poised to recognize and point out areas where workplaces can improve. While autistic people possess unique and highly valuable skills, the "traditional workplace," with its often-unpredictable nature, emphasis on social interaction, potential sensory challenges, and catering to allistic wants and needs, can pose significant barriers to autistic employees (Hendricks, 2010). Job coaching has emerged as a highly effective support strategy in this realm.

With the guidance and on-site support of job coaches, many autistic people can acquire necessary job skills, navigate workplace social scenarios, learn valuable self-advocacy skills, and have an advocate with whom to communicate their needs to their employer (Muller et al., 2008). Beyond this, small yet impactful workplace adjustments can pave the way for success for many autistic people. For example, allowing the use of noise-canceling headphones can mitigate auditory sensory overload, while clear written instructions can provide transparency on tasks and expectations.

Moreover, vocational training programs tailored to the strengths and interests of autistic individuals can prepare them for specific roles in the job market, enhancing their confidence and competence (Hendricks, 2010). An overarching theme in supporting autistic people in the workplace is the importance of clear, straightforward communication. Encouraging employers and co-workers to provide direct feedback and instructions can help to alleviate misunderstandings and foster a more inclusive work environment (Muller et al., 2008).

Navigating the Healthcare and Support Service Systems

Navigating the healthcare system, especially in the United States, can be a complex endeavor for any person. For autistic clients, this process can be particularly challenging due to sensory, communicative, and systemic barriers to access. Mental health professionals play a pivotal role in bridging the gap and ensuring their autistic clients receive appropriate care and support. In this section, we highlight two important intricacies of the healthcare system and medical complex in which mental health professionals may be able to bolster their support for autistic clients: understanding the healthcare system and navigating support service systems.

For many autistic people, the healthcare system presents an overwhelming labyrinth full of barriers that challenge access to care. The first challenge often lies in the sensory environment of healthcare settings. Bright lights, the hum and buzz of medical equipment, and the cacophony of sounds can be distressing for someone with sensory sensitivities (Nicolaidis et al., 2013). Also, misunderstandings and misconceptions about autism by medical professionals can sometimes lead to inadequate or inappropriate care. Communication differences might mean that an autistic person's pain or discomfort is overlooked or misunderstood, leading to diagnostic overshadowing where symptoms are incorrectly attributed to autism rather than a coexisting condition (see Chapter 5 for common co-occurring mental health diagnoses). Here, we list four strategies for support that mental health professionals may target in their work with autistic clients.

First, *enhanced communication.* Mental health professionals should champion the use of clear and concise language, visual aids, hearing aids, communication aids, or alternative communication methods. This might include tools like communication boards, alternative or augmented communication, or apps tailored for healthcare settings. Basic skills training for counselor education can emphasize high levels of eye contact with clients, open-ended questions, and, at times, a veil of expertise. In contrast, some autistic clients could favor less intensive eye contact, more specificity in questions, and explicit explanations for the "hows and whys" of therapy. Second, *sensory accommodation.* Autistic client's healthcare providers should be informed about the need for sensory accommodations, such as providing quiet waiting areas, allowing noise-canceling headphones, reducing ambient sounds (e.g., unnecessary machines, TVs, radios), or using dimmed lights during consultations. Providers should always have fidget items available for client usage. Third, *informed care.* Regular training sessions for healthcare staff can go a long way in dispelling myths about autism. Knowledge about potential co-occurring conditions, sensory needs, and communication styles can lead to better healthcare outcomes. Finally, *patient-centered approaches.* Healthcare providers should be encouraged to allow more extended consultation times,

Table 6.1 Challenges and Strategies in Navigating the Healthcare System for Autistic Clients

Challenge	Description	Strategies for Support
Sensory environment	Overwhelming sensory stimuli (bright lights, loud noises, strong smells, etc.)	Sensory accommodations: quiet waiting areas, noise-canceling headphones, soft (non-fluorescent) lighting
Communication barrier	Miscommunication or misunderstanding due to communication style differences	Enhanced communication: use of visual aids, clear language, alternative communication methods
Inadequate provider understanding	Misconceptions about autism leading to inappropriate care	Informed care: staff autism training, co-occurring condition training, sensory need training
Complex system navigation	Difficulty understanding and navigating healthcare processes	Client-centered approach: extended consultation times, structured routines

ensuring that the autistic patient understands and feels comfortable with the procedures or treatments. This extended time could include structured, predictable routines for transitioning into and out of sessions, given the additional strain of transitions for this population. These interventions may assist autistic clients, and their providers, in understanding the overly complex medical system.

Next, mental health professionals can assist their autistic clients in navigating the complexity of available support services. While there is a plethora of potential services available to autistic clients, the intricate processes involved in actually accessing these services can be confusing and overwhelming. From determining eligibility to navigating support service bureaucracy, autistic clients and their caregivers can often feel lost in a maze (Turcotte et al., 2016). Here, we offer five strategies of support for navigating these systems.

First, *advocacy.* Beyond understanding available services, mental health professionals play a role in advocating for change within the system. This might involve liaising with local and state agencies to streamline processes or increase the availability of necessary services. Clinicians can also help clients to self-advocate by aiding clients in making appointments, preparing for appointments, and processing their experiences after appointments. The Academic Autistic Spectrum Partnership in Research and Education (AASPIRE, n.d.) has created a healthcare toolkit that may assist clinicians and clients in this area (see Appendix D). Second, *clear documentation* (discussed further in Chapter 9). Ensuring that records are up-to-date, organized, and accessible can simplify the process of accessing services. Professionals can assist clients in understanding, completing, and organizing necessary documentation. Third, *collaboration.* By maintaining a strong connection with various service providers, mental health professionals can facilitate smoother transitions, referrals, and coordinated care for their clients. Fourth, *family and caregiver training* (discussed further in Chapter 8). Offering workshops or training sessions for families, or referring out to these, can empower them with the skills and knowledge to advocate for and support their loved ones effectively. This training might cover areas like understanding eligibility criteria, communication strategies, or managing transitions between services. Finally, *feedback mechanisms.* Mental health professionals can encourage the establishment of feedback systems where clients and caregivers can voice their experiences, ensuring continuous improvement in the provision of services.

While understanding and navigating various medical and support systems may be a daunting task, there are pragmatic ways that mental health professionals can support their autistic clients and support systems to ease this burden. A core component of mental health care is client advocacy, and assistance navigating complex systems of support is one way in which mental health professionals can stretch and grow in their advocacy abilities to ensure holistic care for their clients.

Critical Thinking Questions

1. Reflect on the types of sensory accommodations mentioned in educational settings for autistic students, such as fidget tools and quiet areas. How effective do you think these interventions are in promoting academic engagement and success? Are there any additional strategies that could be implemented, considering the sensory and social differences of autistic students?
2. Competitive Integrated Employment (CIE) and sheltered workshops are employment options for autistic people discussed in this chapter. What are the ethical implications of maintaining sheltered workshops that pay below minimum wage, and how does this practice align with or contradict disability justice principles? In what ways might the availability of CIE options challenge or enhance the independence and quality of life of autistic people?
3. Consider the described barriers that autistic clients may face when navigating healthcare systems. What role should mental health professionals play in advocating for systemic changes to healthcare environments and practices? How might the strategies recommended in this chapter be adapted or expanded to address both sensory and communication needs in a way that improves overall healthcare access and outcomes for autistic clients?

7

Working with Families and Caregivers

Learning Outcomes

1. Explore ways in which family narratives and roles can shift following an autism diagnosis.
2. Understand the heritability of autism and the implications of recognizing autistic traits in genetically related family members.
3. Identify strategies for supporting family management of stress and stigma.
4. Explore the importance of a non-judgmental, systemic approach to facilitating family resilience.

Understanding the Family Perspective

Like any aspect of individual experience, autism plays a role in the way in which family systems operate and function. Most research in this area emphasizes the experiences of heterosexual, cisgender couples whose young children receive a formal autism diagnosis. That being said, autism plays a role within every diverse family structure, regardless of the timing, presence, or absence of a diagnosis.

Autism is a highly heritable neurotype, with recent estimated heritability rates at around 80 percent (APA, 2022). Therefore, when an autistic family member is genetically related to other members, it is likely that these other family members may also experience autistic traits. Greater recognition of these autistic traits can lead to self-discovery for these family members. For instance, late-diagnosed adults may discover their own autistic identity through seeing similar qualities or modes of functioning within themselves as their autistic children (Lilley et al., 2022). Similarly, formal diagnoses in the family may lead to recognition of other autistic family members across generations (Lilley et al., 2022). Autistics can feel more comfortable and understood by other autistic individuals in general (Crompton, Hallett, et al., 2020). So later in life, they may also seek out chosen family, including partners, with compatible neurodivergent qualities to their own.

"Broader autism phenotype is a term that has been used to describe common behavioral and cognitive traits associated with autism." Discussions of the population prevalence of autistic traits have pointed to the scholarly disagreement over the term "broader autism phenotype" (Chown, 2019). Scholars have suggested that the term is a misnomer, crafted through semantic obfuscation. Chown (2019) provides evidence to suggest that "autistic traits" clusters (e.g., social communicative needs, cognitive differences, behavioral differences) may be associated with autism, but are not uniquely autistic. Chown suggests that the "broader autism phenotype" arises from one of two categorical errors: "(1) reifying human traits that when clustered together are indicative of someone being autistic, as 'autistic traits'; and (2) regarding certain human traits as pathology in neurodivergent people but as difference in the rest of the general population" (p. 56). While there may be mixed evidence to suggest the reality of the "broader autism phenotype," there may be evidence to suggest the presence of endophenotypes in autism spectrum disorders.

Unlike the "broader autism phenotype" term—which centers on qualitative observable behavior—endophenotypes are quantitative, familial, heritable, measurable genetic markers and indicators of vulnerability to diagnosis which "occupy an intermediate position between genotype and behavior" (Persico & Sacco, 2014, p. 1). In essence, endophenotypes are genetic markers that, in a bottom-up fashion, may contribute to observable behavioral or cognitive traits. In understanding the ways in which "subclinical autism traits" may be experienced and inherited in families, the endophenotype concept holds more empirical ground than "broad autism phenotype." The endophenotype concept has not only been supported in understanding autism traits but also researched in relation to bipolar disorders (e.g., facial emotion labeling deficits in people at risk of bipolar disorders; Brotman et al., 2008) and schizophrenia (e.g., startle reduction and anti-saccade issues in people at risk of schizophrenia spectrum disorders; Greenwood et al., 2019). Movements to understand the genotype-phenotype relationship in autism diagnoses can be helpful in the early recognition of autism.

As discussed in Chapter 3, early recognition of autism plays an important role in a child's growth and development. Diagnosis can also shift family narratives surrounding the life that caregivers imagined for their autistic children (Chiaraluce, 2018). Caregivers can experience anticipation before a diagnosis is received, as well as a grieving process after diagnosis related to said shifting narratives (Bravo-Benítez et al., 2019). Many aspects of family life (e.g., family finances, caregiver occupations, the nature of family outings, and time spent seeking therapeutic care for autistic family members) can shift or change following diagnosis (Chiaraluce, 2018). These shifts and changes can be difficult to navigate.

There are also unique challenges in raising autistic children in a society that often does not value or support disability. Allistic caregivers,

Table 7.1 Differences in Genotype and Phenotype

Genotype	Phenotype
Genetic code:	Physical expression:
	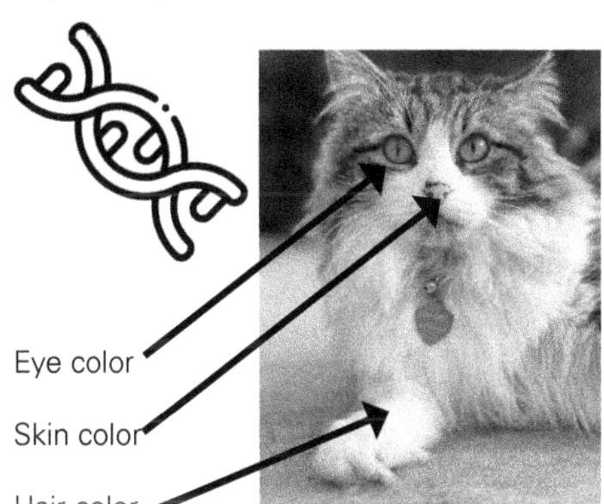

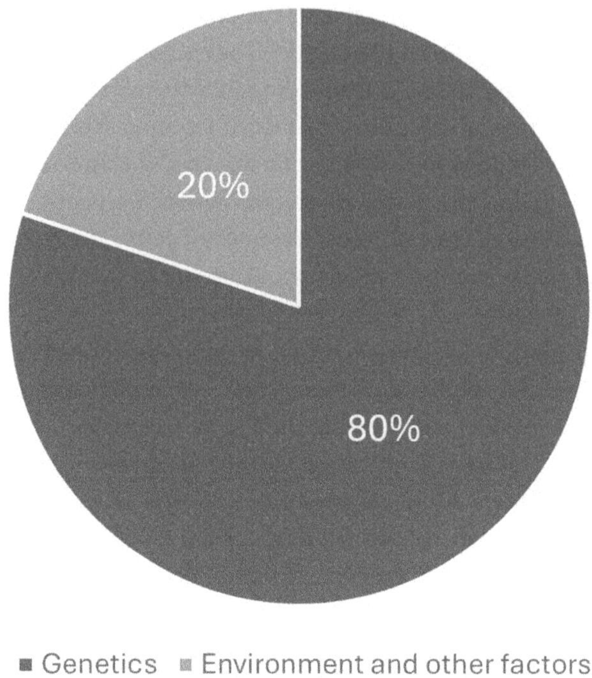

Figure 7.1 Heritability of autism.

autistic children, and allistic siblings experience othering related to external responses to autism (Trew, 2024). Just as autistic individuals experience societal stigma, the caregivers of autistic children can experience affiliate stigma, or stigma related to being associated with a person with a stigmatized identity (Salleh et al., 2020). Caregivers can feel rejected, judged, and embarrassed by the reactions of others toward their autistic children—these reactions can include avoidance, hostile staring, and rude comments (Salleh et al., 2020). Papadopoulos et al. (2018) found a consistent positive relationship between stigma and negative mental health outcomes among caregivers. In a Chinese sample, self-stigma, or the internalization of said stigma by caregivers, has been found to be associated with increased stress over time (Papadopoulos et al., 2019). In turn, this caregiver stress was associated with greater hostility and lower warmth by caregivers toward their children (Papadopoulos et al., 2019). Therefore, identifying and providing support for this stigma is important not only for the health of caregivers but also for their autistic children.

Autistic persons at times also need lifelong support from caregivers, which can also shift the narratives of what these caregivers imagined their life to look like (Williams et al., 2019). Certain autistic support needs have been linked to higher distress. For example, higher behavioral support needs among autistic children are associated with higher stress among caregivers (Kim et al., 2020). Alongside these support needs, caregivers of autistic individuals often lack resources and structural, material support to meet said needs. For instance, there is presently a dearth of housing availability or options for adults with intellectual and developmental disabilities with limited research working to understand these disparities or to identify solutions (Paode, 2020). Autistic parents of autistic children have described a lack of systemic support and a need for systemic change in order to meet their children's needs (Radev et al., 2023).

All of these challenges can be intersectionally impacted by other forms of systemic oppression. For instance, Black caregivers indicated specific stressors including fears surrounding the potential for police violence in response to their autistic children's behaviors, untreated trauma among their children at times compounded by socioeconomic concerns, and difficulty finding support in predominantly White autism community spaces (Dababnah et al., 2022). Immigrant parents of autistic children appear to face specific barriers in navigating service systems in order to meet their children's needs, as well as benefit from healthcare providers helping them to navigate said systems (Wallace-Watkin et al., 2023). Linguistically diverse caregivers face additional barriers in identifying services in their language or with interpreters to meet their needs, instead at times navigating said barriers without support (Wallace-Watkin et al., 2023).

There also appear to be potential differences in relationships between allistic and autistic sibling relationships compared to relationships among allistic siblings. For instance, Tillett and colleagues (2023) found that the relationships between allistic and autistic sibling pairs had lower levels of warmth and intimacy compared to the allistic sibling pairs. The authors argue that these results show the limitations in our current methods of quantitative measurement for capturing the nuances of the relationships of autistic people, given that these measurements were created and normed to understand allistic relationship structures (Tillett et al., 2023). In this viewpoint, autistic relationships are neither better nor worse than allistic relationships but may have differences in the ways in which they show or portray intimacy and warmth, congruent with the Double Empathy Problem. In qualitative research, siblings express desires for supportive spaces for them to process their experiences, as well as support on family conflicts (Trew, 2024).

Family resilience theory investigates the response of family structures to life stressors (Patterson, 2002, as cited in Gunty, 2021). In this theory, the coping response of families to a high number of stressors can result in differential responses, including resilience, which facilitates positive family outcomes (Patterson, 2002, as cited in Gunty, 2021). Family resilience is associated with lower stress for caregivers of autistic children (Kim et al., 2019). However, it is important for providers to recognize that "placing the responsibility for resilience on the family" can include a "lack of awareness of constraints placed on families' abilities to be resilient" (Gunty, 2021, p. 92). In this way, when facilitating support to families of autistic individuals, providers must be aware of systemic barriers toward resilience and provide non-judgmental space for every level of family functioning at treatment onset. In the spirit of a multidisciplinary approach to working with autistic individuals, Tillet and colleagues (2023) suggest that family therapists are poised to be instrumental facilitators of anti-autistiphobic ideology in the therapeutic space—explicitly helping families subvert the Double-Empathy Theory.

Providing Education and Resources

It is important that the family of autistic individuals, including caretakers, have an adequate understanding of autism in order to meet their family member's needs. Aligned with the Double-Empathy Theory as described in Chapter 3, for non-autistic family members, this understanding may not always be intuitive. In fact, misunderstandings between autistic and non-autistic family members have been shown to be influenced by both sides of the relationship (Heasman & Gillespie, 2018).

Aligned with the Social Identity Theory of autism described in Chapter 2 of this guide, caregivers desire for such resources to describe autism as a difference in being with both strengths and challenges (Lodder et al., 2019). Utilizing this approach can allow for autistic family members to be better supported as well as celebrated for their ways of being. It can also help to strengthen family relationships. This is in part because overestimations of social impairments of autistic family members by non-autistic family members are part of what can lead to social misunderstandings (Hearsman & Gillespie, 2017). Therefore, clinicians should carefully consider the lens of the information they provide, favoring resources written by autistic individuals whenever possible. Caregivers have encouraged that resources be provided prior to a formal diagnosis in order to increase understanding of their family experiences sooner rather than later (Lodder et al., 2019).

Alongside information on autism itself, there can also be benefits to providing resources centered on the needs of caregivers or other family members. These additional information sources could include psychoeducation on the impact of stigma against autism on caregivers, ways in which to respond to stigmatizing reactions from others, and avenues for increasing caregiver self-esteem, self-compassion, and resilience (Lodder et al., 2019). Such an approach may also help to combat the Biomedical Model described in Chapter 2 by decentering the autistic person as the diseased party necessitating medical or therapeutic support. Instead, a family approach supports the needs of all members.

Facilitating Family Support Groups

Caregivers of autistic children have identified supportive autism community spaces as important avenues for increasing personal wellbeing (Lodder et al., 2019). Higher emotional support among caregivers is related to reduced stress (Kim et al., 2019). Family support groups are one avenue for providing a space for family members to process their experiences related to the stressors outlined within this section. As mentioned, a clinical diagnosis can result in a grieving process for caregivers related to shifting expectations for who they imagined their autistic child to be (Bravo-Benítez et al., 2019). While all emotional responses deserve space to be felt and processed, it is the responsibility of the group facilitator to provide avenues for processing these responses in a way that is healthy for both the caregiver and their child. Jim Sinclair, an autistic advocate and pioneer for the autism self-advocacy movement, wrote the following in a landmark 1993 piece:

> You didn't lose a child to autism. You lost a child because the child you waited for never came into existence. That isn't the fault of the autistic child who does exist, and it shouldn't be our burden. We need and deserve families who can see us and value us for ourselves, not families whose vision of us is obscured by the ghosts of children who never lived. Grieve if you must, for your own lost dreams. But don't mourn for us. We are alive. We are real. And we're here waiting for you. (Autism is Not Death section, para. 6)

In the same way, facilitators should provide an avenue for caregivers to process their experiences of grief. However, they should also help caregivers to understand their experiences within broader societal ableism. Facilitators can invite non-judgmental introspection into the ways in which ableism can be internalized, as well as the ways in which such internalization can impact broader family structures. Providing this safety for internal exploration within-session could help normalize such responses among group members.

Additionally, providing such a space could help group members to explore nuanced experiences in family dynamics. As mentioned in Chapter 5, autistic individuals have higher rates of trauma-related symptoms (Rumball et al., 2021). Similarly, Andrzejewski and colleagues (2023) explored adverse childhood experiences (ACEs) within dyads comprising autistic children and their parents, comparing these experiences to those of allistic children and their parents. Their findings indicate a significantly higher prevalence of ACEs in dyads of autistic children and their parents when compared to their allistic counterparts. Consequently, these results suggest that group therapy could be helpful in identifying common themes related to the ways in which personal trauma histories influence intergenerational family patterns. This includes insights into the ways in which undiagnosed autism in family members may influence family dynamics. Undertaking such therapeutic interventions is crucial for the well-being of caregivers, family members, and the autistic individuals themselves.

Encouraging Self-Care and Coping Strategies

Beyond formal support, it's important that family members are encouraged to engage in self-care strategies. Among caregivers of autistic children, positive coping strategies are predictive of social support and family quality of life (Wang et al., 2022). In fact, community support, family resilience, and caregiver mental health are positively related, meaning self-care among family members is an important aspect of family well-being (Hayes et al., 2023). Caregivers can experience barriers toward positive emotion-focused coping in line with their life stressors (Williams et al., 2019). Therefore, practitioners should be intentional in helping family members to identify pragmatic self-care strategies that fit their life circumstances and needs. Some examples of coping strategies among caregivers can include physical exercise, leaning on social supports, a spiritual or faith practice, and practicing an attitude of acceptance toward their life circumstances (Williams et al., 2019). Mindfulness has consistently been identified as a specific strategy to positively impact family well-being and stress levels (Cachia et al., 2016). Utilizing this framework, practitioners can help to provide tools that families can integrate into their already existing strategies for family resilience.

Critical Thinking Questions

1. This chapter opens discussion about the ways in which a family member's Autism Spectrum Disorder diagnosis can shift family narratives and even lead other family members to recognize autistic traits within themselves. How might this process of autistic self-recognition among family members impact family relationships and dynamics? What are the potential benefits and challenges of understanding autism as a heritable neurotype in family systems?
2. Family support groups are highlighted as valuable for processing grief and shifting expectations that come with an Autism Spectrum Disorder diagnosis. How can support group facilitators balance allowing caregivers to grieve while also encouraging acceptance, understanding, and celebration of autism as a difference rather than a deficit? In what ways could societal ableism affect caregiver's perceptions, and how can support groups address and mitigate these influences?
3. Given the challenges that caregivers of autistic individuals may face, what are some specific self-care strategies that could be realistically integrated into their routines? How might clinicians support caregivers in identifying and sustaining these self-care practices amid the demands of caregiving?

8

Ethical Considerations and Best Practices

Learning Outcomes

1. Understand the importance of clearly explaining confidentiality and its limitations, with accommodations if needed.
2. Explore practical accommodations to support effective communication and comfort.
3. Reflect upon and acknowledge biases and model ownership of miscommunications.
4. Recognize the importance of ongoing education and staying current with evolving research and best practices in autism support.

Supporting autistic clients requires a deep commitment to ethical principles and best practices. Each of these ensures that the support provided to the client is not only effective, but also respects the rights, dignity, and individuality of each client. These principles are codified, in similar ways, in the ethical codes of many of the major mental health professions in the United States and abroad. For example, the American Psychological Association lists five obligate principles: beneficence and nonmaleficence, fidelity and responsibility, integrity, justice, and respect for people's rights and dignities (APA, 2017). We see these principles echoed in the ethical guidelines from the American Counseling Association: autonomy, nonmaleficence, beneficence, justice, fidelity, and veracity (ACA, 2014). And, finally, an extension of these principles can be seen in the National Association of Social Workers: service, social justice, dignity and worth of the person, importance of human relationships, integrity, and competence (NASW, 2021). In this chapter, we offer suggestions for mental health professionals working with autistic clients across four major ethical and practice domains.

Informed Consent and Confidentiality

Prior to commencing therapeutic treatment, clinicians should ensure that autistic clients have full informed consent. While clinicians should presume capacity to consent unless otherwise proven, they can also provide accommodations to the informed consent process in order to provide additional support (AASPIRE, 2023). One way to accommodate clients is to ensure that all initial paperwork is accessible. The Autism Self-Advocacy Network (2021) has created a resource for converting documents into Easy Read and Plain Language formats for individuals with intellectual and developmental disabilities (see Appendix E). Accessible formatting includes writing in short sentences with one idea per sentence, using clear, unambiguous language, defining all terms utilized, and utilizing bulleted lists or pictorial aids to simplify complex information (ASAN, 2021). Clinicians should also allow for additional time to review documentation with clients if needed by the individual. This process should include an overview of what confidentiality is, how it works, and the limitations to it. Some clients may prefer time to review paperwork prior to appointments so that they have time to formulate and prepare questions ahead of time. Some autistic clients have a legal medical decision maker delineated by an advanced directive (AASPIRE, 2023). In these cases, the preferences and desires of clients toward their care should still be included whenever possible (AASPIRE, 2023). For more information on informed consent for this population, see the AASPIRE Healthcare Toolkit for Patients & Providers in Appendix D.

Respect for Individual Differences and Preferences

Perhaps no ethical area holds greater importance for this population than listening to the needs and desires of each individual client. Healthcare providers often presume they understand the autistic person in front of them, at times rooted in biased assumptions about autism (Nicolaidis et al., 2015). In turn, for autistic people seeking healthcare, difficulty communicating with providers is a common experience (Raymaker et al., 2016). As a result, the needs of autistic individuals can be unmet or undervalued, leading to negative interactions with healthcare settings (Nicolaidis et al., 2015).

Autistic adults identify stress and anxiety, as well as unaccommodating sensory environments, as placing barriers toward their ability to effectively communicate (Cummins et al., 2020). Given the potential for previous negative healthcare interactions among this population, autistic individuals may have founded, congruent reasons for feeling nervous meeting with a new provider for the first time. For all of these reasons, the onus lies with the clinician to ask about their clients' needs and provide accommodations as needed. One initial accommodation that clinics can provide is a text-based method to schedule initial appointments (rather than through phone calls), in alignment with the preference of autistic clients in general (Howard & Sedgewick, 2016). Given the propensity for underdiagnosis and misdiagnosis of autism, all accommodations given to identified autistic clients should also be available to clients in general. Clinicians should also recognize that the individual needs of clients may shift over time or from appointment to appointment, and that autistic individuals may feel more comfortable advocating for their needs when trust and rapport are established in the therapeutic alliance.

Cultural Humility and Sensitivity

As discussed in Chapter 1, when divorced from a biomedical viewpoint, autism can be understood as both a category of individual identity as well as a category of social identity. In alignment with this understanding of autism, Botha and Gillespie-Lynch (2022) argue that "The primary benefit of learning one is autistic is the potential to connect: to the self, to people, to support, and to the world" (p. 104).

Conversely and vitally, to not understand one's autistic identity is to be denied the ability to connect. Among late-diagnosed adults, a common experience is a sense of knowing that one is different from others without knowing the source of the difference (Lupindo et al., 2023). After all, allistic individuals react negatively to autistic individuals upon first interaction (Sasson et al., 2017). With an internalized self-understanding of being "strange," "weird," "off-putting," or "peculiar" to others—in isolation from a community with shared experiences—a person has nowhere to place this difference. Instead, this experience of *individual difference* can be internalized as a matter of *individual wrongness*. The myriad of negative mental health outcomes discussed in Chapter 5 are similarly reflected in the experiences of those who do not know they are autistic until later in life (Lupindo et al., 2023). Among those who understand they are autistic early in life through a biomedical model, the implicit messaging is again that of individual wrongness, with therapies aligned in tandem to correct the error.

Minority stress theory was initially postulated by Meyer (2003) to describe the dual and reciprocal impact of distal (external) stressors and proximal (internal) stressors on the mental health of sexual minorities. When this theory is applied to autistic individuals, psychological distress is similarly predicted by both external experiences of discrimination and internalized stigma against autism (Botha & Frost, 2020). Unlike previous research surrounding the positive impacts of openness about one's queer identity to others, the level of outness about one's autistic identity was predictive of poorer mental health outcomes, perhaps reflecting the ubiquitous nature of social stigma against autism (Botha & Frost, 2020).

Within minority stress theory, community connection and pride are viewed as protective factors against proximal and distal stressors (Meyer, 2003). In the same way, the autistic community facilitates a culture of shared autistic experiences and aims toward social justice (Botha & Gillespie-Lynch, 2022). Through this connection, individual differences can be reframed within a broader sense of communal belonging. This communal belonging does not negate individual disability or individual need, but rather nests individual needs within group affiliation. For instance, online autistic communities reframe understandings of autism from a biomedical model to shared collective experiences—at times in contrast with the aims of allistic researchers attempting to understand autism from an outgroup perspective (Egner, 2022; Guberman, 2023). In turn, a positive sense of autistic identity has consistently been associated with improved mental health outcomes (Davies et al., 2024).

In the same way, allistic allies within the broader autism community should approach their work with autistic clients with a similar attitude of cultural humility (Figure 8.1) that they would approach any diverse population that they are not an individual member of (Davis et al., 2016). To be explicit, this approach to therapy with autistic clients is in many ways subversive to traditional therapeutic paradigms. While a Rogerian approach would acknowledge a client as the expert on their own experiences, mental health professionals are still yet gilded as the experts on individual diagnostic categories. As previously discussed, psychotherapists self-evaluate as having minimal training in

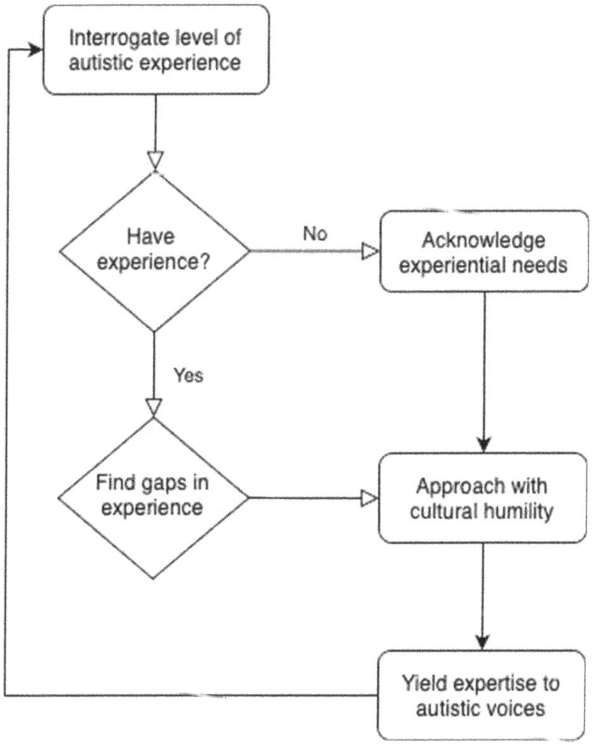

Figure 8.1 Embracing cultural humility when working with autistic clients.

understanding autism (Lipinski, 2022). Therefore, understanding autism from a neurodiversity paradigm means decoupling expertise from allistic professional education and yielding it to communal understandings of autism, as has been recommended for autism researchers (Dinishak & Akhtar, 2022). In doing so, allistic professionals can better identify and celebrate cultural opportunities within sessions to learn more about autism from the experiences of the autistic clients before them (Davis et al., 2018).

In alignment with a multicultural orientation framework, it should also be acknowledged that even with good intentions toward neuro-affirming care, missteps are inevitable. When miscommunications occur, consistent with the Double-Empathy Theory, providers can model taking ownership of their microaggressive actions. Through rupture and repair, providers can facilitate corrective emotional experiences for autistic clients within healthcare settings by recognizing explicitly that communication differences are not the fault of the autistic client.

Alongside these best practices, the autistic community contains the same biases as broader society, meaning it contains and is influenced by social bigotries (Botha & Gillespie-Lynch, 2023). As such, autistic individuals with intersecting marginalized identities experience misunderstandings, microaggressions, and overt discrimination from others in the autistic community. Because of this reality, it is not possible to "challenge neuronormativity without working to undo cisheteronormativity or white supremacy," and a diversity of autistic voices must be uplifted in order to truly support autistic self-advocacy (Botha & Gillespie-Lynch, 2023).

Continuing Education and Professional Development

As with any population with whom we diligently work, continuing professional development is an integral part of the journey. In the spirit of affordable and accessible continuing education and professional development, there are multiple appendices following the references list that point interested readers to various resources. Appendix A includes book recommendations for multiple audiences: clients (of all chronological and developmental ages), mental health professionals, and both. Appendix B includes online periodical suggested reading geared toward enhancing autism understanding in mental health professionals. Appendix C includes some popular online communities for autistic people, which neurotypical clinicians may refer their clients to and neurodivergent clinicians may connect with themselves. Appendix D includes self-diagnosis and skills resources for clients. Clinicians may familiarize themselves with some of these resources, particularly if assessing for autism spectrum disorder. One of our authors, Dr. Chris, has found Embrace Autism quite useful in his own psychological assessment practice. Finally, Appendix E consists of free training in autism and autism spectrum disorder for clinicians. We hope that this list of resources assists you in your continuing educational journey.

The Importance of Ongoing Research and Collaboration

The field of autism research is one that is constantly evolving, and ongoing collaboration between diverse professionals and those with lived experience remains pivotal. Recent studies have emphasized the heterogeneous nature of autism and Autism Spectrum Disorder, discussed at length in the preceding chapters, which suggests that individualized approaches to diagnosis and supportive intervention are crucial for the success of autistic people (Frye et al., 2022). The heterogeneity in autism arises from both the process of diagnosis (including significant changes to psychiatric nosology/classification), and the diverse genetic, neurological, and environmental factors which necessitate a multidisciplinary approach. The complexity of autism highlights the importance of continuous research, not only as a point of advocacy but also to assist practitioners in adapting to the changing paradigms in both medical science and social understanding.

Collaboration among researchers, clinicians, and educators plays a critical role in our understanding of autism. Cross-disciplinary collaborations have led to the development of more effective assessment tools and intervention strategies (Bowman et al., 2021). For instance, the integration of neuroimaging studies into autism evaluation has increased the predictive validity of autism assessment for a neurotype that has largely been assessed and intervened reactively (Ayoub et al., 2022). International collaborations have also become increasingly significant in understanding autism, as they allow for a more diverse range of data—encompassing different genetic backgrounds and cultural contexts—which is crucial for understanding a neurotype that is globally prevalent (Zeidan et al., 2022).

Finally, perhaps one of the most important advances in autism research is the involvement of autistic individuals and their families in the research process. This shift toward an ontological valuing of autistic experience is more inclusive and holistic than the systematic ignoring of autistic lived experiences. This participatory research model not only ensures that the research is aligned with the actual needs of the autism community but also helps in dismantling misconceptions, stereotypes, and stigma associated with autism and Autism Spectrum Disorder (Keating, 2021). The authors of this current text hope that, through the continued collaborative efforts of autistic and allistic researchers, educators, clinicians, and advocates, we continue to steer toward a future of understanding, inclusion, and celebration of all neurotypes.

Critical Thinking Questions

1. Reflect on the ethical principles discussed in this chapter—autonomy, justice, respect for dignity—in relation to informed consent practices for autistic clients. How might clinicians ensure that the principles are upheld while providing necessary accommodations? What particular challenges might arise during this process, and how can they be addressed to support a truly client-centered approach?
2. How does the concept of cultural humility apply directly and uniquely within the context of neurodiversity and autism? What steps can clinicians take to better understand, and challenge, their own biases? How might this self-reflection enhance therapeutic relationships and outcomes with autistic clients?

3. Involving autistic people in research and professional development about autism has been considered a point of epistemic justice. What are the ethical implications of this inclusive approach to field development? How might collaborative research between autistic people, researchers, clinicians, and educators transform traditional views of autism? What barriers might exist to implementing this model widely, and how might invested parties overcome those barriers to create more representative and inclusive research?

Glossary

Activities of daily living (ADLs) Essential and routine tasks related to personal care, including ambulating, feeding, dressing, personal hygiene, continence, and toileting (Edemekong et al., 2023).

Alexithymia A difficulty identifying and describing internal emotional states in relation to physical bodily cues. An experience more common (but not universal) among autistic individuals compared to allistic individuals (Kinnaird et al., 2019).

Augmentative and alternative communication (AAC) An umbrella term for communication devices utilized by non-speaking (or temporarily non-speaking) autistic individuals encompassing several different modalities ranging from high to low tech.

Autigender An autistic-specific gender identity where the individual's experience of or understanding towards their gender is in some way tied to or in other cases intrinsically related to their experience of autism. May be an identity in relation to other gender(s) or a standalone identity.

Autistic burnout An autism-specific mental health condition characterized by persistent exhaustion, increases in executive functioning concerns, perceived increases in autistic traits, and withdrawal from social and other activities (Arnold et al., 2023). An indication of long unmet needs and/or unsupportive life environments/circumstances.

Autistic inertia An autistic executive functioning concern related to difficulty with task initiation, task switching, and task interruption in spite of internal efforts (Buckle et al., 2021).

Body-Focused Repetitive Behaviors (BRFBs) An umbrella term for compulsive behaviors targeting one's physical state, including hair pulling (trichotillomania), skin picking (excoriation), lip biting, cheek biting, etc. (APA, 2022). Classified under obsessive-compulsive and related disorders when at the level of clinical significance, meaning the individual has tried multiple times to decrease the behavior(s), which cause significant distress in daily living (APA, 2022). Distinctive from non-suicidal self-injury (NSSI).

Camouflaging (masking) A conscious or unconscious strategy toward minimizing autistic traits. Can include compensatory strategies (such as consciously mirroring one's conversational partner, increasing eye contact) and masking external autistic traits (such as decreasing stimming behaviors, reducing autistic communication strategies) (Hull et al., 2017).

Double-empathy theory A theory that recognizes autistic and allistic communication strategies are not better or worse, but rather that a mismatch can occur on both ends of communication. Instead, societally, autistic communication is pathologized, while allistic communication is normalized (Milton, 2013).

Dyscalculia A math learning disability that impairs an individual's number sense, often including the learning of number-related concepts, performing calculations, reasoning, and problem-solving.

Dysgraphia A writing learning disability that impacts an individual's abilities to turn thoughts into written language, often including difficulties with fine motor skills, spatial perception, language processing, and orthographic coding.

Dyslexia A reading learning disability that impacts an individual's abilities to process written language, often including spelling, learning letters and their sounds, and reading.

Dyspraxia A movement disability that impacts an individual's coordination, often including balance, posture, motor sequencing, and fine motor skills.

Echolalia The repetition of words or phrases, often spoken by another person, occurs frequently in autism. Echolalia can be immediate or delayed, communicative or semi-communicative, mitigated or non-mitigated, and person-directed or non-person directed (Patra & Jesus, 2023).

Exteroception Perception of external sensory information. Related to sensory processing concerns in autistic individuals.

Hyperfocus An energized, intensive, sustained focus on a topic of interest that can last between hours to several days common among autistic individuals and ADHDers.

Individualized education program (IEP) A tailored approach to teaching, learning, and assessment, ensuring that the student's needs are met (Whitaker, 2007).

Infodumping An autistic conversational strategy marked by high levels of information sharing on a topic of interest, often with enthusiasm or excitement.

Interoception Perception of internal bodily processes, queues, or needs (Noel et al., 2018). Autistic individuals could have difficulties identifying physical needs related to areas like hunger, thirst, pain, or toileting in relation to interoception concerns.

Meltdown An intense, external release of overwhelming emotions during which individuals can feel out of control and/or experience cognitive disorganization; triggered by preceding stressors (such as sensory overload, schedule changes, etc.) (Lewis & Stevens, 2023).

Monotropism An autistic cognitive style marked by a tendency toward narrowed, detail-oriented focus (Murray et al., 2005).

Neuroqueer A noun, verb, and adjective dependent upon context which positions or understands queerness and neurodiversity as intertwined. Can be or describe a social identity or include practices toward said identity (Walker, 2021).

Non-speaking Not verbalizing language, instead speaking through other means that do not utilize the voice (e.g., sign language, augmentative and alternative communication).

Proprioception Kinesthetic awareness of bodily position in relation to the environment. Related to autistic individuals' sense of bodily awareness, embodiment, and physical movement (Welch et al., 2021).

Savantism Describes the experience present in about 10 percent of autistic individuals in which one skill set or area of knowledge is perceived by others as a pronounced area of aptitude related to the spiky profile of the individual (Treffert et al., 2009).

Scripting An aspect of camouflaging through which individuals spend time and efforts in preparation for upcoming social interactions, ranging from physically written word-for-word scripts to mental rehearsal of potential conversation topics (Hull et al., 2017).

Sensory overload A state of overwhelm related to discomforting sensory information, potentially leading to meltdowns or shutdowns. See **meltdown**.

Sensory-seeking behavior Desiring or moving toward activities with high levels of sensory stimulation in order to meet sensory needs. Examples could include eating spicy foods, listening to loud music, or riding roller coasters.

Shutdown A highly emotionally intensive and/or overwhelming internalized response to a buildup of external stressors, potentially accompanied by increased sensory sensitivity. See sensory overload; meltdown

Special interest A focal point of autistic cognitive attention on a specific topic or area. Can be pursued with a monotropic (tunneling, inward) focus. A source of joy and meaning-making in life, as well as an avenue for connecting with others. See **monotropism**.

Spiky profile A visual representation of the unique strengths and challenges of a singular autistic individual which helps to portray the complexity and non-linearity underlying the wide array of skills, experiences, and challenges associated with autism.

Stimming A regulatory self-soothing strategy utilizing sensory stimulation such as sights, sounds, smells, textures, or vestibular movements. At times observable by external repetitive behaviors including hand movements, vocalizations, and chewing behaviors. At other times an internal experience not observable by others. See **sensory-seeking behavior**.

Appendix A
Book Recommendations

For Clinicians

1. Hartman et al. (2022). *The Adult Autism Assessment Handbook: A Neurodiversity-Affirmative Approach.* https://uk.jkp.com/products/the-adult-autism-assessment-handbook
2. Marschall, A. (2024). *A Clinician's Guide to Supporting Autistic Clients: Over 100 Treatment Recommendations and Interventions for Creating a Neurodiversity-Affirming Practice.* https://catalog.pesi.com/item/a-clinicians-guide-supporting-autistic-clients-131859

For Clients

1. Wylie (2014). *Very Late Diagnosis of Asperger Syndrome (Autism Spectrum Disorder): How Seeking a Diagnosis in Adulthood Can Change Your Life.* https://uk.jkp.com/products/very-late-diagnosis-of-asperger-syndrome-autism-spectrum-disorder?_pos=1&_sid=1c327e612&_ss=r
2. McCreary (2019). *Funny, You Don't Look Autistic: A Comedian's Guide to Life on the Spectrum.* https://www.annickpress.com/Books/F/Funny-You-Don-t-Look-Autistic
3. Hirschy & Greenberg (2023). *My Autistic Mama.* https://a.co/d/1MzPduA
4. Hammond & Cosgrove (2023). *A Day with No Words.* https://a.co/d/fYHQ4wI
5. Alcott (2021). *When Things Get Too Loud.* https://a.co/d/6TqUjhE

6. Marschall & Lastowski (2023). *Slipper the Penguin.* https://a.co/d/2ukjqN2
7. The Autism Self-Advocacy Network (2020). *Welcome to the Autistic Community.* https://autisticadvocacy.org/book/welcome-to-the-autistic-community/

For Both

1. Cook & Purkis (2022). *The Autism and Neurodiversity Self-Advocacy Handbook: Developing Skills to Determine Your Own Future.* https://uk.jkp.com/products/the-autism-and-neurodiversity-self-advocacy-handbook?_pos=1&_sid=b27f47686&_ss=r
2. Price (2022). *Unmasking Autism: Discovering the New Faces of Neurodiversity.* https://www.penguinrandomhouse.com/books/688819/unmasking-autism-by-devon-price-phd/
3. Silberman (2015). *NeuroTribes: The Legacy of Autism and the Future of Neurodiversity.* https://www.penguinrandomhouse.com/books/310415/neurotribes-by-steve-silberman-foreword-by-oliver-sacks/
4. Omeiza (2023). *Autistic and Black: Our Experiences of Growth, Progress and Empowerment.* https://www.hennesseyingalls.com/book/9781839976209
5. Mendes, E. A. & Maroney, M. R. (2019). *Gender identity, sexuality, and autism: Voices from across the spectrum.* Jessica Kingsley Publishers. https://us.jkp.com/products/gender-identity-sexuality-and-autism
6. Kapp, S. (2020). *Autistic Community and the Neurodiversity Movement: Stories from the Frontline.* https://link.springer.com/book/10.1007/978-981-13-8437-0

Appendix B
Online Periodical Suggested Reading

1. Lewis (2020). Autism Is an Identity, Not a Disease: Inside the Neurodiversity Movement. https://elemental.medium.com/autism-is-an-identity-not-a-disease-inside-the-neurodiversity-movement-998ecc0584cd
2. Vance (2021). The Identity Theory of Autism: How Autistic Identity Is Experienced Differently. https://neuroclastic.com/the-identity-theory-of-autism-how-autistic-identity-is-experienced-differently/
3. Marschall (2022). What Does It Mean for a Therapist to Be Neurodiversity-Affirming? https://www.verywellmind.com/what-does-it-mean-for-a-therapist-to-be-neurodiversity-affirming-6829954
4. Lowry, M. (2023). AUCT- Autistic Centered Therapy. https://www.mattlowrylpp.com/blog/auct-autistic-centered-therapy
5. Natri (2021). How and Why Neurotypicals Misunderstand and Mistreat Autistic People. https://www.madinamerica.com/2021/10/neurotypicals-misunderstand-mistreat-autistic-people/
6. Botha and Gillespie-Lynch (2022). Come as You Are: Examining Autistic Identity Development and the Neurodiversity Movement through an Intersectional Lens. https://psycnet.apa.org/record/2022-65128-004

Appendix C
Online Communities for Autistic Clients

- BlueSky
  - #AutSci
  - #actuallyautistic
- Mastodon
  - disabled.social
  - neurodifferent.me
- Reddit
  - https://reddit.com/autism
  - https://reddit.com/autisminwomen
  - https://reddit.com/autismtranslated
- Wrong Planet
  - https://wrongplanet.net

Appendix D

Self-Diagnosis and Skill Resources for Clients

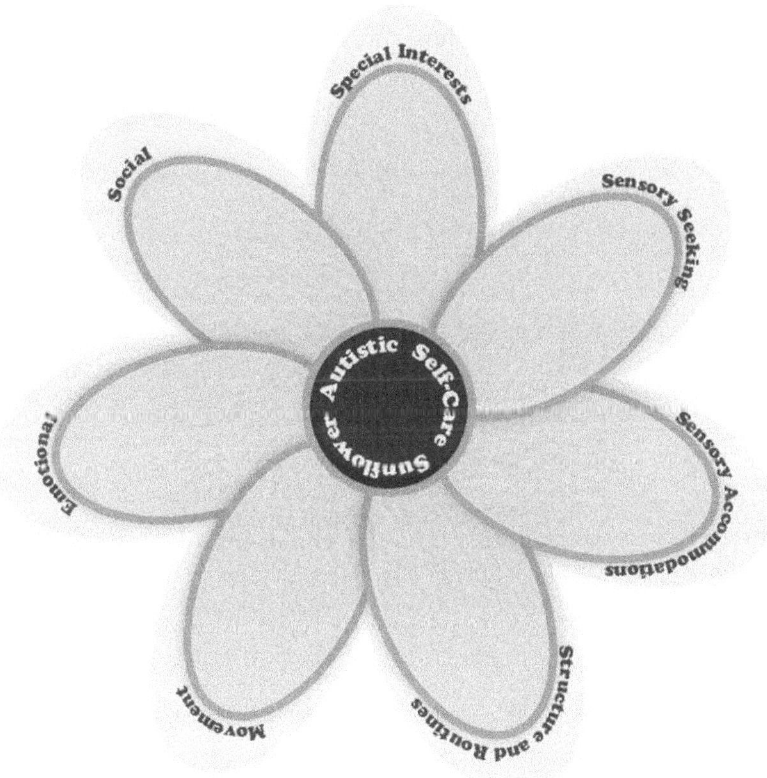

Figure D.1 The Autistic Self-Care Sunflower allows clients to identify areas of self-care in a variety of areas related to autistic well-being.

1. Autistic's Guide to Adulthood's online, self-paced, life skills resource: https://autisticsguide.org.au
2. Autistics Unmasked Self-Evaluation Guide: https://autisticsunmasked.org/am-i-autistic/
3. Neurodivergent Insights: The Alexithymia Workbook: https://neurodivergentinsights.com/emotions/alexithymia-workbook/
4. AASPIRE Healthcare Toolkit for Patients & Providers: https://autismandhealth.org/?a=pt&p=main&t=pt_frm&theme=ltlc&size=small
5. The Neurodivergent Friendly Workbook of DBT Skills - digital version: https://www.livedexperienceeducator.com/store
6. Autistic Self-Care Sunflower

Appendix E

Free Training and Professional Development in Autism

1. **University of Missouri, Thompson Center for Autism & Neurodevelopment** offers five modules covering a variety of topics about autism: young children, screening, transition to adulthood, and others. https://thompsoncenter.missouri.edu/autism-training/online-training-modules/
2. **OpenLearn** hosts an eight-week introductory training program about autism, including diagnostics, support needs, lifespan development, potential causes, and historical information. https://www.open.edu/openlearn/science-maths-technology/understanding-autism/content-section-overview?active-tab=description-tab
3. **The Autism Certification Center** offers a paid certification. However, anyone can freely access the ninety-minute module *Many Faces of Autism*, which dispels common myths about autism through interviews with autistic people. It also offers some practical strategies for helping autistic folks. Click "Get Started" on the following link: https://autismcertificationcenter.org/course-guide/many-faces-autism
4. **The Autistic Self-Advocacy Network** hosts *One Idea Per Line: A Guide to Making Easy Read Resources*, a guide created to help with formatting documents and resources in an accessible way for clients with IDD. https://autisticadvocacy.org/wp-content/uploads/2021/07/One-Idea-Per-Line.pdf

5. **Stimpunks Foundation** has developed a self-directed course, *Neurodiversity and Gender: Queer and Neurodivergent Liberation are Entwined*, which elaborates on the relationship between gender diversity and neurodiversity. https://stimpunks.org/courses/neurodiversity-and-gender/

References

Academic Autistic Spectrum Partnership in Research and Education. (n.d.). *AASPIRE healthcare toolkit: Primary care resources for adults on the autism spectrum and their primary care providers.* Retrieved from https://autismandhealth.org/

Allison C., Auyeung B., & Baron-Cohen S. (2012). Toward brief "red flags" for autism screening: The short autism spectrum quotient and the short quantitative checklist in 1,000 cases and 3,000 controls. *Journal of the American Academy of Child & Adolescent Psychiatry, 51*, 202–212.

Amaral, D. G. (2017). Examining the causes of autism. *Cerebrum: The Dana Forum on Brain Science.* https://journals.scholarsportal.info/details/15246205/v2017inone/nfp_etcoa.xml

American Counseling Association. (2014). 2014 ACA code of ethics. https://www.counseling.org/docs/default-source/default-document-library/ethics/2014-aca-code-of-ethics.pdf

American Psychiatric Association. (2022). *Diagnostic and statistical manual of mental disorders* (5th ed., text rev.). https://doi.org/10.1176/appi.books.9780890425787

American Psychological Association. (2017). Ethical principles of psychologists and code of conduct (2002, amended effective June 1, 2010, and January 1, 2017). https://www.apa.org/ethics/code/

American Speech-Language-Hearing Association. (2024). *Echolalia and its role in gestalt language acquisition.* American Speech-Language-Hearing Association. https://www.asha.org/practice-portal/clinical-topics/autism/echolalia-and-its-role-in-gestalt-language-acquisition/#:~:text=Echolalia%20is%20the%20repetition%20of,or%20after%20a%20brief%20delay

Anderson, L. K. (2023). Autistic experiences of applied behavior analysis. Autism, 27(3), 737-750. https://doi.org/10.1177/13623613221118216

Andrzejewski, T., DeLucia, E. A., Semones, O., Khan, S., & McDonnell, C. G. (2023). Adverse childhood experiences in autistic children and their caregivers: Examining intergenerational continuity. *Journal of Autism and Developmental Disorders, 53*(7), 2663–2679. https://doi.org/10.1007/s10803-022-05551-w

Arnevik, E. A., & Helverschou, S. B. (2016). Autism Spectrum Disorder and co-occurring Substance Use Disorder – A systematic review. *Substance Abuse: Research and Treatment, 10*, SART.S39921. https://doi.org/10.4137/SART.S39921

Arnold, S. R., Higgins, J. M., Weise, J., Desai, A., Pellicano, E., & Trollor, J. N. (2023). Towards the measurement of autistic burnout. *Autism, 27*(7), 1933–1948. https://doi.org/10.1177/13623613221147400

Ashburner, J., Ziviani, J., & Rodger, S. (2010). Surviving in the mainstream: Capacity of children with autism spectrum disorders to perform academically and regulate their emotions and behavior at school. *Research in Autism Spectrum Disorders, 4*(1), 18–27. https://doi.org/10.1016/j.rasd.2009.07.002

Au-Yeung, S. K., Bradley, L., Robertson, A. E., Shaw, R., Baron-Cohen, S., & Cassidy, S. (2019). Experience of mental health diagnosis and perceived misdiagnosis in autistic, possibly autistic and non-autistic adults. *Autism, 23*(6), 1508–1518. https://doi.org/10.1177/1362361318818167

Autistic Self-Advocacy Network. (2021). One idea per line: A guide to making easyread resources. Retrieved from https://autisticadvocacy.org/wp-content/uploads/2021/07/One-Idea-Per-Line.pdf

Ayoub, M. J., Keegan, L., Tager-Flusberg, H., & Gill, S. V. (2022). Neuroimaging techniques as descriptive and diagnostic tools for infants at risk for autism spectrum disorder: A systematic review. *Brain Sciences, 12*(5), 602. https://doi.org/10.3390/brainsci12050602

Bagatell, N. (2010). From cure to community: Transforming notions of autism. *Ethos, 38*(1), 33–55. https://doi.org/10.1111/j.1548-1352.2009.01080.x

Bagby, R. M., Parker, J. D. A., & Taylor, G. J. (1994). The twenty-item Toronto Alexithymia Scale-I. Item selection and cross-validation of the factor structure. *Journal of Psychosomatic Research, 38*, 23–32.

Baio, J., Wiggins, L., Christensen, D. L., Maenner, M. J., Daniels, J., Warren, Z., Kurzius-Spencer, M., Zahorodny, W., Robinson Rosenberg, C., White, T., Durkin, M. S., Imm, P., Nikolaou, L., Yeargin-Allsopp, M., Lee, L. C., Harrington, R., Lopez, M., Fitzgerald, R. T., Hewitt, A., Pettygrove, S., Constantino, J. N., Vehorn, A., Shenouda, J., Hall-Lande, J., Van Naarden Braun, K., & Dowling, N. F. (2018). Prevalence of autism spectrum disorder among children aged 8 years - Autism and Developmental Disabilities Monitoring Network, 11 Sites, United States, 2014. *Morbidity and mortality weekly report, surveillance summaries, 67*(6), 1–23. https://doi.org/10.15585/mmwr.ss6706a1

Beaton, D. M., Sirois, F., & Milne, E. (2022). Experiences of criticism in adults with ADHD: A qualitative study. *PLoS ONE, 17*(2). https://doi.org/10.1371/journal.pone.0263366

Bellini, S., Peters, J. K., Benner, L., & Hopf, A. (2007). A meta-analysis of school-based social skills interventions for children with autism spectrum disorders. *Remedial and Special Education*, *28*(3), 153–162. https://doi.org/10.1177/07419325070280030401

Biel, L. (2017). Sensory corner: Fidget toys or focus tools? *Sensory Smarts*, 12–13. https://www.sensorysmarts.com/AADJun17.pdf

Bird, G., & Cook, R. (2013). Mixed emotions: the contribution of alexithymia to the emotional symptoms of autism. Translational psychiatry, 3(7), e285–e285. https://doi.org/10.1038/tp.2013.61

Black, M. H., Mahdi, S., Milbourn, B., Scott, M., Gerber, A., Esposito, C., Falkmer, M., Lerner, M. D., Halladay, A., Ström, E., D'Angelo, A., Falkmer, T., Bölte, S., & Girdler, S. (2020). Multi-informant international perspectives on the facilitators and barriers to employment for autistic adults. *Autism Research, 13*(7), 1195–1214. https://doi.org/10.1002/aur.2288

Botha, M., & Gillespie-Lynch, K. (2022). Come as you are: Examining autistic identity development and the neurodiversity movement through an intersectional lens. Human Development, 66(2), 93-112. https://doi.org/10.1159/000524123

Botha, M., & Frost, D. M. (2020). Extending the minority stress model to understand mental health problems experienced by the autistic population. Society and mental health, 10(1), 20-34. https://doi.org/10.1177/2156869318804297

Bottema-Beutel, K., & Crowley, S. (2021). Pervasive undisclosed conflicts of interest in applied behavior analysis autism literature. Frontiers in Psychology, 12, 676303. https://doi.org/10.3389/fpsyg.2021.676303

Bowman, K. S., Suarez, V. D., & Weiss, M. J. (2021). Standards for interprofessional collaboration in the treatment of individuals with autism. *Behavior Analysis in Practice*, *14*(4), 1191–1208. https://doi.org/10.1007/s40617-021-00560-0

Bowri, M., Hull, L., Allison, C., Smith, P., Baron-Cohen, S., Lai, M.-C., & Mandy, W. (2021). Demographic and psychological predictors of alcohol use and misuse in autistic adults. *Autism, 25*(5), 1469–1480. https://doi.org/10.1177/1362361321992668

Bravo-Benítez, J., Pérez-Marfil, M. N., Román-Alegre, B., & Cruz-Quintana, F. (2019). Grief experiences in family caregivers of children with autism spectrum disorder (ASD). *International Journal of Environmental Research and Public Health, 16*(23), 4821. https://doi.org/10.3390/ijerph16234821

Brickhill, R., Atherton, G., Piovesan, A., & Cross, L. (2023). Autism, thy name is man: Exploring implicit and explicit gender bias in autism perceptions. *PLoS One, 18*(8), e0284013. https://doi.org/10.1371/journal.pone.0284013

Brooke, V., Brooke, A. M., Schall, C., Wehman, P., McDonough, J., Thompson, K., & Smith, J. (2018). Employees with autism spectrum disorder achieving long-term employment success: A retrospective review of employment retention and intervention. Research and Practice for Persons with Severe Disabilities, 43(3), 181–193. https://doi.org/10.1177/1540796918783202

Brotman, M. A., Guyer, A. E., Lawson, E. S., Horsey, S. E., Rich, B. A., Dickstein, D. P., Pine, D. S., & Leibenluft, E. (2008). Facial emotion labeling deficits in children and adolescents at risk for bipolar disorder. *The American Journal of Psychiatry, 165*(3), 385–389. https://doi.org/10.1176/appi.ajp.2007.06122050

Brown, C. M., Attwood, T., Garnett M., & Stokes, M. A. (2020). 'Am I Autistic? Utility of the Girls Questionnaire for Autism Spectrum Condition as an Autism Assessment in Adult Women. *Autism In Adulthood, 2* (3), 216–226. http://doi.org/10.1089/aut.2019.0054

Brown, C. M., Hedley, D., Hooley, M., Hayward, S. M., Fuller-Tyszkiewicz, M., Krug, I., & Stokes, M. A. (2024). Hiding in plain sight: Eating disorders, autism, and diagnostic overshadowing in women. *Autism in Adulthood.* https://doi.org/10.1089/aut.2023.0197

Brown, F., Michaels, C. A., Oliva, C. M., & Woolf, S. B. (2008). Personal paradigm shifts among ABA and PBS experts: Comparisons in treatment acceptability. Journal of Positive Behavior Interventions, 10(4), 212–227. https://doi.org/10.1177/1098300708318799

Bruce, H., Munday, K., & Kapp, S. K. (2023). Exploring the experiences of autistic transgender and non-binary adults in seeking gender identity health care. *Autism in Adulthood, 5*(2), 191–203. http://doi.org/10.1089/aut.2023.0003

Brugha, T. S., McManus, S., Bankart, J., Scott, F., Purdon, S., Smith, J., Bebbington, P., Jenkins, R., & Meltzer, H. (2011). Epidemiology of autism spectrum disorders in adults in the community in England. *Archives of General Psychiatry, 68*(5), 459–466. https://doi.org/10.1001/archgenpsychiatry.2011.38

Buckle, K. L., Leadbitter, K., Poliakoff, E., & Gowen, E. (2021). "No way out except from external intervention": First-hand accounts of autistic inertia. *Frontiers in Psychology, 12,* 1592. https://doi.org/10.3389/fpsyg.2021.631596

Buijsman, R., Begeer, S., & Scheeren, A. M. (2022). 'Autistic person' or 'person with autism'? Person-first language preference in Dutch adults with autism and parents. *Autism, 27*(3), 788–795. https://doi.org/10.1177/13623613221117914

Bury, S. M., Jellett, R., Spoor, J. R., & Hedley, D. (2023). "It defines who I am" or "It's something I have": What language do [autistic] Australian adults [on the autism spectrum] prefer? *Journal of Autism and Developmental Disorder, 53,* 677–687. https://doi.org/10.1007/s10803-020-04425-3

Bureau of Labor Statistics. (2025). Persons with a disability: Labor force characteristics—2024. U.S. Department of Labor. Retrieved from https://www.bls.gov/news.release/pdf/disabl.pdf

Butler, L. D., Critelli, F. M., & Rinfrette, E. S. (2011). Trauma-informed care and mental health. *Directions in Psychiatry, 31*(3), 197–212.

Butwicka, A., Långström, N., Larsson, H., Lundström, S., Serlachius, E., Almqvist, C., Frisén, L., & Lichtenstein, P. (2017). Increased risk for substance use-related problems in Autism Spectrum Disorders: A population-based cohort study. *Journal of Autism and Developmental Disorders, 47*(1), 80–89. https://doi.org/10.1007/s10803-016-2914-2

Cachia, R. L., Anderson, A., & Moore, D. W. (2016). Mindfulness, stress and well-being in parents of children with autism spectrum disorder: A systematic review. *Journal of Child and Family Studies, 25*, 1–14. https://doi.org/10.1007/s10826-015-0193-8

Calisan Kinter, R., Ozbaran, B., Inal Kaleli, I., Kose, S., Bildik, T., & Ghaziuddin, M. (2024). The sensory profiles, eating behaviors, and quality of life of children with autism spectrum disorder and avoidant/restrictive food intake disorder. *Psychiatric Quarterly*, 1–22. https://doi.org/10.1007/s11126-023-10063-6

Case-Smith, J., & Arbesman, M. (2008). Evidence-based review of interventions for autism used in or of relevance to occupational therapy. *American Journal of Occupational Therapy, 62*(4), 416–429. https://doi.org/10.5014/ajot.62.4.416.

Cervantes, P. E., & Matson, J. L. (2015). Comorbid symptomology in adults with autism spectrum disorder and intellectual disability. Journal of Autism and Developmental Disorders, 45, 3961–3970. https://doi.org/10.1007/s10803-015-2553-z

Chan, K. K. S., Yip, C. C. H., & Leung, D. C. K. (2023). Longitudinal impact of self-stigma content and process on parental warmth and hostility among parents of children with autism spectrum disorder. *Journal of Autism and Developmental Disorders, 53*(7), 2728–2736. https://doi.org/10.1007/s10803-022-05529-8

Charlton, R. A., Entecott, T., Belova, E., & Nwaordu, G. (2021). "It feels like holding back something you need to say": Autistic and Non-Autistic Adults accounts of sensory experiences and stimming. *Research in Autism Spectrum Disorders, 89*, 101864. https://doi.org/10.1016/j.rasd.2021.101864

Chiaraluce, C. A. (2018). Narratives on the autism journey:"Doing family" and redefining the caregiver self. Journal of Family Issues, 39(10), 2883–2905. https://doi.org/10.1177/0192513X18765048

Chown, N. (2019). Are the "autistic traits" and "broader autism phenotype" concepts real or mythical?. *Autism Policy and Practice, 2*(1), 46–63. https://www.openaccessautism.org/index.php/app

Cimera, R. E., Wehman, P., West, M., & Burgess, S. (2012). Do sheltered workshops enhance employment outcomes for adults with autism spectrum disorder?. *Autism, 16*(1), 87–94. https://doi.org/10.1177/1362361311408

Clin, E., & Kissine, M. (2023). Neurotypical, but not autistic, adults might experience distress when looking at someone avoiding eye contact: A live face-to-face paradigm. *Autism, 27*(7), 1949–1959. https://doi.org/10.1177/13623613221148553

Conner, C. M., & White, S. W. (2018). Brief report: Feasibility and preliminary efficacy of individual mindfulness therapy for adults with autism spectrum disorder. *Journal of Autism and Developmental Disorders, 48*(1), 290–300. https://doi.org/10.1007/s10803-017-3312-0

Cook, J., Crane, L., Bourne, L., Hull, L., & Mandy, W. (2021). Camouflaging in an everyday social context: An interpersonal recall study. *Autism*, 25(5), 1444–1456. https://doi.org/10.1177/1362361321992641

Cooper, R., Cooper, K., Russell, A. J., & Smith, L. G. (2021). "I'm proud to be a little bit different": The effects of autistic individuals' perceptions of autism and autism social identity on their collective self-esteem. *Journal of Autism and Developmental Disorders*, 51, 704–714. http://doi.org/10.1007/s10803-020-04575-4 https://doi.org/10.1177/13623613211004328

Cooper, K., Russell, A. J., Lei, J., & Smith, L. G. (2023). The impact of a positive autism identity and autistic community solidarity on social anxiety and mental health in autistic young people. *Autism, 27*(3), 848–857. https://doi.org/10.1177/13623613221118351

Costache, M. E., Gioia, F., Vanello, N., Greco, A., Lefebvre, F., Capobianco, A., ... & Weiner, L. (2024). Exploring emotion control and alexithymia in Autistic Adults: An ecological momentary assessment study. *Journal of Autism and Developmental Disorders*, 1–15. http://doi.org/10.1007/s10803-024-06551-8

Coupland, J. (2003). Small talk: Social functions. *Research on Language and Social Interaction, 36*(1), 1–6. https://doi.org/10.1207/S15327973RLSI3601_1

Crane, L., Hearst, C., Ashworth, M., Davies, J., & Hill, E. L. (2021). Supporting newly identified or diagnosed autistic adults: An initial evaluation of an autistic-led programme. *Journal of Autism and Developmental Disorders, 51*, 892–905. http://doi.org/10.1007/s10803-020-04486-4

Crane, L., Goddard, L., & Pring, L. (2009). Sensory processing in adults with autism spectrum disorders. *Autism, 13*(3), 215–228. https://doi.org/10.1177/1362361309103794

Crompton, C. J., Hallett, S., Ropar, D., Flynn, E., & Fletcher-Watson, S. (2020). "I never realised everybody felt as happy as I do when I am around autistic people': A thematic analysis of autistic adults" relationships with autistic and neurotypical friends and family. *Autism, 24*(6), 1438–1448. https://doi.org/10.1177/1362361320908976

Crompton, C. J., Ropar, D., Evans-Williams, C. V., Flynn, E. G., & Fletcher-Watson, S. (2020). Autistic peer-to-peer information transfer is highly effective. *Autism, 24*(7), 1704–1712. https://doi.org/10.1177/1362361320919286

Crompton, C. J., Sharp, M., Axbey, H., Fletcher-Watson, S., Flynn, E. G., & Ropar, D. (2020). Neurotype-matching, but not being autistic, influences self and observer ratings of interpersonal rapport. *Frontiers in Psychology, 11*. https://doi.org/10.3389/fpsyg.2020.586171

Cummins, C., Pellicano, E., & Crane, L. (2020). Autistic adults' views of their communication skills and needs. *International Journal of Language & Communication Disorders, 55*(5), 678–689. https://doi.org/10.1111/1460-6984.12552

Dababnah, S., Kim, I., & Shaia, W. E. (2022). "I am so fearful for him": A mixed-methods exploration of stress among caregivers of Black children with autism. *International Journal of Developmental Disabilities, 68*(5), 658–670. https://doi.org/10.1080/20473869.2020.1870418

Dabbs, C. R., Hutchins, C. H., Baird, R., Scaer, A. J., Kosanovich, S. E., & Spitler-Nigh, B. (2024). Unmasking bias: Autistic perspectives in mental health training. *Autism in Adulthood.* Advance online publication. https://doi.org/10.1089/aut.2024.0210

Dallman, A. (2024). Affective contact in autism: A phenomenological study of the emotional experiences of autistic adults. *The American Journal of Occupational Therapy, 78*(4), 7804205070. https://doi.org/10.5014/ajot.2024.050502

Darazsdi, Z., & Bialka, C. S. (2023). "Oh, you couldn't be autistic": Examining anti-autistic bias and self-esteem in the therapeutic alliance. *Autism, 27*(7), 2124–2134. http://doi.org/10.1177/13623613231154622

Davies, J., Cooper, K., Killick, E., Sam, E., Healy, M., Thompson, G., Mandy, W., Redmayne, B., & Crane, L. (2024). Autistic identity: A systematic review of quantitative research. *Autism Research*, 1–24. https://doi.org/10.1002/aur.3105

Davis, D. E., DeBlaere, C., Brubaker, K., Owen, J., Jordan, T. A., Hook, J. N., & Van Tongeren, D. R. (2016). Microaggressions and perceptions of cultural humility in counseling. Journal of Counseling & Development, 94(4), 483-493. https://doi.org/10.1002/jcad.12107

de Bruin, E. I., Blom, R., Smit, F. M., Van Steensel, F. J., & Bögels, S. M. (2015). MYmind: Mindfulness training for youngsters with autism spectrum disorders and their parents. *Autism, 19*(8), 906–914. https://doi.org/10.1177/1362361314553279

Devita-Raeburn, E. (2016, August 10). *The controversy over autism's most common therapy.* Spectrum News. https://www.spectrumnews.org/features/deep-dive/controversy-autisms-common-therapy/

Dinishak, J., & Akhtar, N. (2023). Integrating autistic perspective into autism science: A role for autistic autobiographies. *Autism, 27*(3), 578–587. https://doi.org/10.1177/13623613221123731

Doyle, N., McDowall, A., & Waseem, U. (2022). Intersectional stigma for autistic people at work: A compound adverse impact effect on labor force participation and experiences of belonging. *Autism in Adulthood, 4*(4), 340–356. https://doi.org/10.1089/aut.2021.008

DuBay, M., Watson, L., & Zhang, W. (2019). In search of culturally appropriate autism interventions: Perspective of Latino caregivers. *Journal of Autism and Developmental Disorders, 48*(5), 1623–1639. https://doi.org/10.1007/s10803-017-3394-8

Duncan, A. W., & Bishop, S. L. (2015). Understanding the gap between cognitive abilities and daily living skills in adolescents with autism spectrum disorders with average intelligence. *Autism: The International Journal of Research and Practice, 19*(1), 64–72. https://doi.org/10.1177/1362361313510068

Dwyer, P. (2022). The neurodiversity approach(es): What are they and what do they mean for researchers? *Human Development, 66*(2), 73–92. https://doi.org/10.1159/000523723

Edemekong, P. F., Bomgaars, D. L., Sukumaran, S., & Schoo, C. (2023). Activities of daily living. In Treasure Island (FL): StatPearls Publishing; 2023 Jan-. https://www.ncbi.nlm.nih.gov/books/NBK470404/

Egan, V., Linenberg, O., & O'Nions, E. (2019). The measurement of adult pathological demand avoidance traits. *Journal of Autism and Developmental Disorders, 49*, 481–494. https://doi.org/10.1007/s10803-018-3722-7

Egner, J. (2022). # ActuallyAutistic: Using Twitter to construct individual and collective identity narratives. Studies in Social Justice, 16(2), 349–369. https://doi.org/10.26522/ssj.v16i2.2675

Engel, G. L. (1977). The need for a new medical model: a challenge for biomedicine. *Science, 196*(4286), 129-136.

Eriksson, J. M., Andersen, L. M., & Bejerot, S. (2013). RAADS-14 Screen: Validity of a screening tool for autism spectrum disorder in an adult psychiatric population. *Molecular Autism, 4*, 1–11. https://doi.org/10.1186/2040-2392-4-49

ESpecialNeeds. (2024). *Adaptive communication switches.* ESpecialNeeds.com. https://www.especialneeds.com/shop/assistive-technology/switches.html

Etyemez, S., Esler, A., Kini, A., Tsai, P. C., DiRienzo, M., Maenner, M., & Lee, L. C. (2022). The role of intellectual disability with autism spectrum disorder and the documented cooccurring conditions: A population-based study. Autism Research, 15(12), 2399–2408. https://doi.org/10.1002/aur.2831

Frye, R. E., Rose, S., Boles, R. G., & Rossignol, D. A. (2022). A personalized approach to evaluating and treating autism spectrum disorder. *Journal of Personalized Medicine, 12*(2), 147. https://doi.org/10.3390/jpm12020147

Fulton, R., Reardon, E., Kate, R., & Jones, R. (2020). Sensory trauma: Autism, sensory difference and the daily experience of fear. Autism Wellbeing CIC. https://www.researchgate.net/publication/351918786_Sensory_Trauma_-_autism_sensory_difference_and_the_daily_experience_of_fear

Fusar-Poli, L., Brondino, N., Politi, P., & Aguglia, E. (2022). Missed diagnoses and misdiagnoses of adults with autism spectrum disorder. *European Archives of Psychiatry and Clinical Neuroscience, 272*(2), 187–198. https://doi.org/10.1007/s00406-020-01189-w

Gerhardt, P. F., Cicero, F., & Mayville, E. (2014). Employment and related services for adults with autism spectrum disorders. In F. Volkmar, B. Reichow, & J. C. McPartland (Eds.), *Adolescents and adults with autism spectrum disorders.* (pp. 105–119). Springer. http://doi.org/10.1007/978-1-4939-0506-5

Gesi, C., Migliarese, G., Torriero, S., Capellazzi, M., Omboni, A. C., Cerveri, G., & Mencacci, C. (2021). Gender differences in misdiagnosis and delayed diagnosis among adults with autism spectrum disorder with no language or intellectual disability. *Brain Sciences, 11*(7), 912. https://doi.org/10.3390/brainsci11070912

Gillespie-Lynch, K., Kapp, S. K., Brooks, P. J., Pickens, J., & Schwartzman, B. (2017). Whose expertise is it? Evidence for autistic adults as critical autism experts. Frontiers in Psychology, 8, 438. https://doi.org/10.3389/fpsyg.2017.00438

Goodwin, J., Gordon, I., O'Keeffe, S., Carling, S., Berresford, A., Bhattarai, N., . . . & Cassidy, S. (2024). Adapting safety plans for autistic adults with involvement from the autism community. *Autism in Adulthood.* Advance online publication. https://doi.org/10.1089/aut.2023.0124

Grant, J. E., & Chamberlain, S. R. (2022). Autistic traits in trichotillomania. *Brain and Behavior, 12*(7). https://doi.org/10.1002/brb3.2663

Gray, C. A., & Garand, J. D. (1993). Social stories: Improving responses of students with autism with accurate social information. *Focus on Autistic Behavior, 8*(1), 1–10. https://doi.org/10.1177/108835769300800l

Greenwood, T. A., Shutes-David, A., & Tsuang, D. W. (2019). Endophenotypes in schizophrenia: Digging deeper to identify genetic mechanisms. *Journal of Psychiatry and Brain Science, 4*(2). https://doi.org/10.20900/jpbs.20190005

Grinker, R. R. (2020). Autism,"stigma," disability: A shifting historical terrain. *Current Anthropology, 61*(S21), S55–S67. https://doi.org/10.1086/705748

Guberman, J. (2023). # ActuallyAutistic Twitter as a site for epistemic resistance and crip futurity. ACM Transactions on Computer-Human Interaction, 30(3), 1-34. https://doi.org/10.1145/3569891

Gunty, A. L. (2021). Rethinking resilience in families of children with autism spectrum disorders. Couple and Family Psychology: Research and Practice, 10(2), 87–102. https://doi.org/10.1037/cfp0000155

Hadjikhani, N., Åsberg Johnels, J., Zürcher, N.R., Lassalle, A., Guillon, Q., Hippolyte, L., Billstedt, E., Ward, N., Lemonnier, E., & Gillberg, C. (2017). Look me in the eyes: Constraining gaze in the eye-region provokes abnormally high subcortical activation in autism. *Scientific Reports, 7,* 3163. https://doi.org/10.1038/s41598-017-03378-5

Halim, A. T., Richdale, A. L., & Uljarević, M. (2018). Exploring the nature of anxiety in young adults on the autism spectrum: A qualitative study. *Research in Autism Spectrum Disorders, 55,* 25–37. https://doi.org/10.1016/j.rasd.2018.07.006

Hammond, E. (2023). *Differences in Autistic and NT communication styles. TeachersPayTeachers.com.* https://www.teacherspayteachers.com/Product/Differences-in-Autistic-and-NT-communication-styles-9-page-infographic-9079365

Hassen, N. B., Molins, F., Garrote-Petisco, D., & Serrano, M. A. (2023). Emotional regulation deficits in autism spectrum disorder: The role of alexithymia and interoception. *Research in Developmental Disabilities, 132,* 104378. https://doi.org/10.1016/j.ridd.2022.104378

Hartley, G., Sirois, F., Purrington, J., & Rabey, Y. (2024). Adverse childhood experiences and autism: A meta-analysis. *Trauma, Violence, & Abuse, 25*(3), 2297–2315. https://doi.org/10.1177/15248380231213314

Hartman, L. M., Farahani, M., Moore, A., Manzoor, A., & Hartman, B. L. (2023). Organizational benefits of neurodiversity: Preliminary findings on autism and the bystander effect. *Autism Research, 16*(10), 1989–2001. https://doi.org/10.1002/aur.3012

Haruvi-Lamdan, N., Horesh, D., Zohar, S., Kraus, M., & Golan, O. (2020). Autism spectrum disorder and post-traumatic stress disorder: An unexplored co-occurrence of conditions. *Autism, 24*(4), 884–898. https://doi.org/10.1177/1362361320912143

Hayes, K. N., Rossetti, K. G., & Zlomke, K. (2023). Community support, family resilience and mental health among caregivers of youth with autism spectrum disorder. *Child: Care, Health and Development, 49*(1), 130–136. https://doi.org/10.1111/cch.13025

Heasman, B., & Gillespie, A. (2018). Perspective-taking is two-sided: Misunderstandings between people with asperger's syndrome and their family members. *Autism, 22*(6), 740–750. https://doi.org/10.1177/1362361317708287

Hendricks, D. (2010). Employment and adults with autism spectrum disorders: Challenges and strategies for success. *Journal of Vocational Rehabilitation, 32*(2), 125–134. https://doi.org/10.3233/JVR-2010-0502

Holingue, C., Newill, C., Lee, L. C., Pasricha, P. J., & Daniele Fallin, M. (2018). Gastrointestinal symptoms in autism spectrum disorder: A review of the literature on ascertainment and prevalence. *Autism Research, 11*(1), 24–36. https://doi.org/10.1002/aur.1854

Howard, P. L., & Sedgewick, F. (2021). 'Anything but the phone!': Communication mode preferences in the autism community. *Autism, 25*(8), 2265–2278. https://doi-org.argo.library.okstate.edu/10.1177/13623613211014995

Hull, L., Mandy, W., Lai, M. C., Baron-Cohen, S., Allison, C., Smith, P., & Petrides, K. V. (2019). Development and validation of the camouflaging autistic traits questionnaire (CAT-Q). *Journal of Autism and Developmental Disorders, 49*, 819–833. https://doi.org/10.1007/s10803-018-3792-6

Hull, L., Levy, L., Lai, M. C., Petrides, K. V., Baron-Cohen, S., Allison, C., ... & Mandy, W. (2021). Is social camouflaging associated with anxiety and depression in autistic adults?. *Molecular Autism*, 12, 1-13. https://doi.org/10.1186/s13229-021-00421-1

Hull, L., Petrides, K. V., Allison, C., Smith, P., Baron-Cohen, S., Lai, M. C., & Mandy, W. (2017). "Putting on my best normal": Social camouflaging in adults with autism spectrum conditions. Journal of Autism and Developmental Disorders, 47, 2519-2534. https://doi.org/10.1007/s10803-017-3166-5

Hull, L., Rane, S., Lee, S. H. L., & Sedgewick, F. (2024). "Just ask what support we need": Autistic adults' feedback on social skills training. *Autism in Adulthood.* https://doi.org/10.1089/aut.2023.0136

Jadav, N., & Bal, V. H. (2022). Associations between co-occurring conditions and age of autism diagnosis: Implications for mental health training and adult autism research. *Autism Research, 15*(11), 2112–2125. https://doi.org/10.1002/aur.2808

Jaswal, V. K., & Akhtar, N. (2018). Being versus appearing socially uninterested: Challenging assumptions about social motivation in autism. *Behavioral and Brain Sciences, 42,* e82. http://doi.org/10/1017/S0140525X18001826

Kapp, S.K. (2020). Introduction. In: Kapp, S. (eds) *Autistic Community and the Neurodiversity Movement.* Palgrave Macmillan, Singapore. https://doi.org/10.1007/978-981-13-8437-0_1

Kapp, S. K., Gillespie-Lynch, K., Sherman, L. E., & Hutman, T. (2013). Deficit, difference, or both? Autism and neurodiversity. *Developmental Psychology, 49*(1), 59–71. https://doi.org/10.1037/a0028353

Kapp, S. K., Steward, R., Crane, L., Elliott, D., Elphick, C., Pellicano, E., & Russell, G. (2019). 'People should be allowed to do what they like': Autistic adults' views and experiences of stimming. *Autism, 23*(7), 1782–1792. https://doi.org/10.1177/1362361319829628

Keating, C. T. (2021). Participatory autism research: How consultation benefits everyone. *Frontiers in Psychology, 12.* https://doi.org/10.3389/fpsyg.2021.713982

Kentrou, V., Livingston, L. A., Grove, R., Hoekstra, R. A., & Begeer, S. (2024). Perceived misdiagnosis of psychiatric conditions in autistic adults. *EClinicalMedicine, 71.* https://doi.org/10.1016/j.eclinm.2024.102586

Kildahl, A. N., Helverschou, S. B., Bakken, T. L., & Oddli, H. W. (2020). "If we do not look for it, we do not see it": Clinicians' experiences and understanding of identifying post-traumatic stress disorder in adults with autism and intellectual disability. *Journal of Applied Research in Intellectual Disabilities*, 33(5), 1119–1132. https://doi.org/10.1111/jar.12734

Kiehl, I., Pease, R., & Hackmann, C. (2024). The adult experience of being diagnosed with autism spectrum disorder: A qualitative meta-synthesis. *Autism, 28*(5), 1060–1074. https://doi.org/10.1177/13623613231220419

Kim, I., Dababnah, S., & Lee, J. (2020). The influence of race and ethnicity on the relationship between family resilience and parenting stress in caregivers of children with autism. *Journal of Autism and Developmental Disorders, 50*(2), 650–658. https://doi.org/10.1007/s10803-019-04269-6

Kimber, L., Verrier, D., & Connolly, S. (2023). Autistic people's experience of empathy and the autistic empathy deficit narrative. *Autism in Adulthood*. Advance online publication. https://doi.org/10.1089/aut.2023.0001

Kinnaird, E., Stewart, C., & Tchanturia, K. (2019). Investigating alexithymia in autism: A systematic review and meta-analysis. *European Psychiatry, 55*, 80–89. http://doi.org/10.1016/j.eurpsy.2018.09.004

Koenig, K. P., Buckley-Reen, A., & Garg, S. (2012). Efficacy of the Get Ready to Learn yoga program among children with autism spectrum disorders: A pretest–posttest control group design. *American Journal of Occupational Therapy, 66*(5), 538–546. https://doi.org/10.5014/ajot.2012.004390

Koffer Miller, K. H., Mathew, M., Nonnemacher, S. L., & Shea, L. L. (2018). Program experiences of adults with autism, their families, and providers: Findings from a focus group study. *Autism, 22*(3), 345–356. https://doi.org/10.1177/1362361316679000

Koomar, T., Thomas, T. R., Pottschmidt, N. R., Lutter, M., & Michaelson, J. J. (2021). Estimating the prevalence and genetic risk mechanisms of ARFID in a large autism cohort. *Frontiers in Psychiatry, 12*. https://doi.org/10.3389/fpsyt.2021.668297

Kouijzer, M. E. J., de Moor, J. M. H., Gerrits, B. J. L., Congedo, M., & van Schie, H. T. (2009). Neurofeedback improves executive functioning in children with autism spectrum disorders. *Research in Autism Spectrum Disorders, 3*(1), 145–162. https://doi.org/10.1016/j.rasd.2008.05.001

Kulawiak, P. R. (2021). Academic benefits of wearing noise-cancelling headphones during class for typically developing students and students with special needs: A scoping review. *Cogent Education, 8*(1). https://doi.org/10.1080/2331186X.2021.1957530

Kupferstein, H. (2018). Evidence of increased PTSD symptoms in autistics exposed to applied behavior analysis. *Advances in Autism, 4*(1), 19–29. https://doi.org/10.1108/AIA-08-2017-0016

Kushki, A., Anagnostou, E., Hammill, C., Duez, P., Brian, J., Iaboni, A., Schachar, R., Crosbie, J., Arnold, P., & Lerch, J. P. (2019). Examining overlap and homogeneity in ASD, ADHD, and OCD: a data-driven, diagnosis-agnostic approach. *Translational Psychiatry, 9*(1), 318. https://doi.org/10.1038/s41398-019-0631-2

Lai, M.-C., Kassee, C., Besney, R., Bonato, S., Hull, L., Mandy, W., Szatmari, P., & Ameis, S. H. (2019). Prevalence of co-occurring mental health diagnoses in the autism population: A systematic review and meta-analysis. *The Lancet Psychiatry, 6*(10), 819–829. https://doi.org/10.1016/S2215-0366(19)30289-5

Lai, M.-C., Lombardo, M. V., Auyeung, B., Chakrabarti, B., & Baron-Cohen, S. (2015). Sex/gender differences and autism: Setting the scene for future research. *Journal of the American Academy of Child & Adolescent Psychiatry, 54*(1), 11–24. http://doi.org/10.1016/j.jaac.2014.10.003

Lewis, L. F., & Stevens, K. (2023). The lived experience of meltdowns for autistic adults. *Autism, 27*(6), 1817–1825. https://doi.org/10.1177/13623613221145783

Libster, N., Knox, A., Engin, S., Geschwind, D., Parish-Morris, J., & Kasari, C. (2022). Personal victimization experiences of autistic and non-autistic children. *Molecular Autism, 13*(1), 51. https://doi.org/10.1186/s13229-022-00531-4

Lilley, R., Lawson, W., Hall, G., Mahony, J., Clapham, H., Heyworth, M., ... & Pellicano, E. (2022). 'A way to be me': Autobiographical reflections of autistic adults diagnosed in mid-to-late adulthood. Autism, 26(6), 1395–1408. https://doi.org/10.1177/13623613211050694

Lilley, R., Lawson, W., Hall, G., Mahony, J., Clapham, H., Heyworth, M., Arnold, S., Trollor, J., Yudell, M., & Pellicano, E. (2023). "Peas in a pod": Oral history reflections on autistic identity in family and community by late-diagnosed adults. *Journal of Autism and Developmental Disorders, 53*, 1146–1161. https://doi.org/10.1007/s10803-022-05667-z

Lime Network. (n.d.). "Leading perspectives on disability: a Q&A; with Dr. Stephen Shore." *Lime Network.* Archived at *Wayback Machine* (www.webarchive.org/) > https://web.archive.org/web/20201205094047/https://limeconnect.com/opportunities_news/detail/leading-perspectives-on-disability-a-qa-with-dr-stephen-shore

Lipinski, S., Boegl, K., Blanke, E. S., Suinkel, U., & Dziobek, I. (2022). A blind spot in mental healthcare? Psychotherapists lack education and expertise for the support of adults on the autism spectrum. *Autism, 26*(6), 1509–1521. https://doi.org/10.1177/13623613211057973

Livingston, L. A., Shah, P., & Happé, F. (2019). Compensatory strategies below the behavioural surface in autism: A qualitative study. The Lancet Psychiatry, 6(9), 766–777. http://doi.org/10.1016/S2215-0366(19)30224-X

Locke, J., Osuna, A., Myrvold, R. J., & Closson, J. S. (2024). Supporting autistic college students: Examining the Mentoring, Organization and Social Support for Autism Inclusion on Campus (MOSSAIC) Program. *Journal of Autism and Developmental Disorders, 54*(6), 2094–2107. http://doi.org/10.1007/s10803-023-05969-w

Lodder, A., Papadopoulos, C., & Randhawa, G. (2019). The development of a stigma support intervention to improve the mental health of family carers of autistic children: Suggestions from the autism community. *European*

Journal of Mental Health, 14(1), 58–77. https://doi.org/10.5708/EJMH.14.2019.1.4

Long, H., Cooper, K., & Russell, A. (2024). 'Autism is the Arena and OCD is the Lion': Autistic adults' experiences of co-occurring obsessive-compulsive disorder and repetitive restricted behaviours and interests. *Autism*, 28(11), 2897–2908. https://doi.org/10.1177/13623613241251512

Long, H., Cooper, K., & Russell, A. (2024). 'Autism is the Arena and OCD is the Lion': Autistic adults' experiences of co-occurring obsessive-compulsive disorder and repetitive restricted behaviours and interests. *Autism*, 13623613241251512. https://doi.org/10.1177/13623613241251512

Lord, C., Risi, S., DiLavore, P. S., Shulman, C., Thurm, A., & Pickles, A. (2006). Autism from 2 to 9 years of age. *Archives of General Psychiatry, 63*(6), 694–701. https://doi.org/10.1001/archpsyc.63.6.694

Lugo-MarÍn, J., Magán-Maganto, M., Rivero-Santana, A., Cuéllar-Pompa, L., Alviani, M., Jenaro-Río, C., Díez, E., & Canal-Bedia, R. (2019). Prevalence of psychiatric disorders in adults with autism spectrum disorder: A systematic review and meta-analysis. *Research in Autism Spectrum Disorders, 59*(1), 22–33. https://doi.org/10.1016/j.rasd.2018.12.004

Lundström, S., Chang, Z., Kerekes, N., Gumpert, C. H., Råstam, M., Gillberg, C., . . . & Anckarsäter, H. (2011). Autistic-like traits and their association with mental health problems in two nationwide twin cohorts of children and adults. *Psychological Medicine, 41*(11), 2423–2433. https://doi.org/10.1017/S0033291711000377

Lupindo, B. M., Maw, A., & Shabalala, N. (2023). Late diagnosis of autism: Exploring experiences of males diagnosed with autism in adulthood. Current Psychology, 42(28), 24181–24197. https://doi.org/10.1007/s12144-022-03514-z

McDonald, T. A. M. (2020). Autism identity and the "Lost Generation": Structural validation of the Autism Spectrum Identity Scale and comparison of diagnosed and self-diagnosed adults on the autism spectrum. *Autism in Adulthood, 2*(1), 13–23. https://doi.org/10.1089/aut.2019.0069

McGill & Robison, 2020:McGill, O., & Robinson, A. (2020). "Recalling hidden harms": Autistic experiences of childhood applied behavioural analysis (ABA). Advances in Autism, 7(4), 269-282. https://doi.org/10.1108/AIA-04-2020-0025

Maddox, B. B., Crabbe, S. R., Fishman, J. M., Beidas, R. S., Brookman-Frazee, L., Miller, J. S., Nicolaidis, C., & Mandell, D. S. (2019). Factors influencing the use of cognitive-behavioral therapy with autistic adults.

Journal of Autism and Developmental Disorders, 49, 4421–4428. https://doi.org/10.1007/s10803-019-04156-0

Maddox, B. B., Crabbe, S., Beidas, R. S., Brookman-Frazee, L., Cannuscio, C. C., Miller, J. S., ... & Mandell, D. S. (2020). "I wouldn't know where to start": Perspectives from clinicians, agency leaders, and autistic adults on improving community mental health services for autistic adults. *Autism, 24*(4), 919-930. https://doi.org/10.1177/1362361319882227

Maddox, B. B., & White, S. W. (2015). Comorbid social anxiety disorder in adults with autism spectrum disorder. *Journal of Autism and Developmental Disorders, 45*, 3949–3960. https://doi.org/10.1007/s10803-015-2531-5

Maenner, M. J., Warren, Z., Williams, A. R., Amoakohene, E., Bakian, A. V., Bilder, D. A., Durkin, M. S., Fitzgerald, R.T., Furnier, S. M., Hughes, M. M., Ladd-Acosta, C. M., McArthur, D., Pas, E. T., Salinas, A., Vehorn, A., Williams, S., Esler, A., Grzybowski, A., Hall-Lande, J., Nguyen, R. H. N., Pierce, K., Zahorodny, W., Hudson, A., Hallas, L., Mancilla, K.S., Patrick, M., Shenouda, J., Sidwell, K., DiRienzo, M., Gutierrez, J., Spivey, M. H., Lopez, M., Pettygrove, S., Schwenk, Y. D., Washington, A., & Shaw, K. A. (2023). Prevalence and characteristics of autism spectrum disorder among children aged 8 years—Autism and Developmental Disabilities Monitoring Network, 11 sites, United States, 2020. *MMWR Surveillance Summaries, 72*(No. SS-2), 1–14. http://doi.org/10.15585/mmwr.ss7202a1

Maitland, C. A., Rhodes, S., O'Hare, A., & Stewart, M. E. (2021). Social identities and mental well-being in autistic adults. *Autism*, 25(6), 1771–1783. https://doi.org/10.1177/13623613211004328

Malone, K. M., Pearson, J. N., Palazzo, K. N., Manns, L. D., Rivera, A. Q., & Mason Martin, D. L. (2022). The scholarly neglect of black autistic adults in autism research. *Autism in Adulthood, 4*(4), 271–280. http://doi.org/10.1089/aut.2021.0086

Mandell, D. S., Listerud, J., Levy, S. E., & Pinto-Martin, J. A. (2002). Race differences in the age at diagnosis among Medicaid-eligible children with autism. *Journal of the American Academy of Child & Adolescent Psychiatry, 41*(12), 1447–1453. http://doi.org/10.1097/00004583-200212000-00016

Mathur, S. K., Renz, E., & Tarbox, J. (2024). Affirming neurodiversity within applied behavior analysis. *Behav Analysis Practice*. https://doi.org/10.1007/s40617-024-00907-3

Matson, J. L., Worley, J.A., Fodstad, J. C., Chung, K-M., Suh, D., Jhin, H. K., Ben-Itzchak, E., Zachor, D. A., & Furniss, F. (2011). A multinational study examining the cross cultural differences in reported symptoms of autism spectrum disorders: Israel, South Korea, the United Kingdom, and the

United States of America. *Research in Autism Spectrum Disorders, 5*(4), 1598–1604. https://doi.org/10.1016/j.rasd.2011.03.007

Mayes, S. D., & Zickgraf, H. (2019). Atypical eating behaviors in children and adolescents with autism, ADHD, other disorders, and typical development. *Research in Autism Spectrum Disorders, 64*, 76–83. https://doi.org/10.1016/j.rasd.2019.04.002

Mazurek, M. O. (2014). Loneliness, friendship, and well-being in adults with autism spectrum disorders. *Autism, 18*(3), 223–232. https://doi.org/10.1177/1362361312474121

Mazurek, M. O., Lu, F., Macklin, E. A., & Handen, B. L. (2019). Factors associated with DSM-5 severity level ratings for autism spectrum disorder. *Autism, 23*(2), 468–476. https://doi.org/10.1177/1362361318755318

McConnell, E. A., & Minshew, R. (2023). Feminist therapy at the intersection of gender diversity and neurodiversity. *Women & Therapy, 46*(1), 36–57. https://doi.org/10.1080/02703149.2023.2189776

McCrossin R. (2022). Finding the true number of females with autistic spectrum disorder by estimating the biases in initial recognition and clinical diagnosis. *Children (Basel, Switzerland), 9*(2), 272. https://doi.org/10.3390/children9020272

McQuaid, G. A., Strang, J. F., & Jack, A. (2024). Borderline personality as a factor in late, missed, and mis-diagnosis in autistic girls and women: A conceptual analysis. *Autism in Adulthood.* Advance online publication. https://doi.org/10.1089/aut.2023.0034

Meier, S. M., Petersen, L., Schendel, D. E., Mattheisen, M., Mortensen, P. B., & Mors, O. (2015). Obsessive-compulsive disorder and autism spectrum disorders: longitudinal and offspring risk. *PloS ONE, 10*(11), e0141703. http://doi.org/10.1371/journal.pone.0141703

Meyer, I. H. (2003). Prejudice, social stress, and mental health in lesbian, gay, and bisexual populations: Conceptual issues and research evidence. Psychological Bulletin, 129(5), 674–697. https://doi.org/10.1037/0033-2909.129.5.674

Milton, D. (2013). "Natures answer to over-conformity": Deconstructing pathological demand avoidance. *Kent Academic Repository,* 1–11. https://kar.kent.ac.uk/62694/

Milton, D. E. (2012). On the ontological status of autism: The 'double empathy problem'. Disability & Society, 27(6), 883-887. https://doi.org/10.1080/09687599.2012.710008

Milton, D., Gurbuz, E., & López, B. (2022). The "double empathy problem": Ten years on. *Autism, 26*(8), 1901–1903. https://doi.org/10.1177/13623613221129123

Moore, R., & Friedman, M. (2017). The role of informed choice in advancing competitive integrated employment. *Journal of Vocational Rehabilitation, 46*(2), 245–264. http://doi.org/10.3233/JVR-160860

Müller, E., Schuler, A., & Yates, G. B. (2008). Social challenges and supports from the perspective of individuals with asperger syndrome and other autism spectrum disabilities. *Autism, 12*(2), 173–190. https://doi.org/10.1177/1362361307086664

Murray, A. L., Booth, T., Auyeung, B., McKenzie, K., & Kuenssberg, R. (2019). Investigating sex bias in the AQ-10: A replication study. *Assessment, 26*(8), 1474–1479. https://doi.org/10.1177/1073191117733548

Murray, D., Lesser, M., & Lawson, W. (2005). Attention, monotropism and the diagnostic criteria for autism. *Autism, 9*(2), 139–156. https://doi.org/10.1177/1362361305051398

Nader, A. M., Courchesne, V., Dawson, M., & Soulières, I. (2016). Does WISC-IV underestimate the intelligence of autistic children? Journal of Autism and Developmental Disorders, 46, 1582–1589. https://doi.org/10.1007/s10803-014-2270-z

National Association of Social Workers. (2017). NASW code of ethics. https://www.socialworkers.org/About/Ethics/Code-of-Ethics/Code-of-Ethics-English

Newell, V., Phillips, L., Jones, C., Townsend, E., Richards, C., & Cassidy, S. (2023). A systematic review and meta-analysis of suicidality in autistic and possibly autistic people without co-occurring intellectual disability. *Molecular Autism, 14*(1), 1–37. https://doi.org/10.1186/s13229-023-00544-7

Nicolaidis, C., Raymaker, D., McDonald, K., Dern, S., Boisclair, W. C., Ashkenazi, E., & Baggs, A. (2013). Comparison of healthcare experiences in autistic and non-autistic adults: A cross-sectional online survey facilitated by an academic-community partnership. *Journal of General Internal Medicine, 28*(6), 761–769. https://doi.org/10.1007/s11606-012-2262-7

Nicolaidis, C., Raymaker, D. M., McDonald, K. E., Baggs, A. E., Dern, S., Kapp, S. K., Weiner, M., Boisclair, W. C., & Ashkenazy, E., (2015). "Respect the way I need to communicate with you": Healthcare experiences of adults on the autism spectrum. *Autism, 19*(7), 824–831. http://doi.org/10.1177/1362361315576221

NLA Stage 1. (2022). Communication Development Center. https://communicationdevelopmentcenter.com/nlp-stage-1/

Noel, J. P., Lytle, M., Cascio, C., & Wallace, M. T. (2018). Disrupted integration of exteroceptive and interoceptive signaling in autism spectrum disorder. *Autism Research, 11*(1), 194–205. http://doi.org/10.1002/aur.1880

Obsessions and repetitive behavior - A guide for all audiences. (n.d.). The National Autistic Society. https://www.autism.org.uk/advice-and-guidance/topics/behaviour/obsessions/all-audiences#:~:text=Many%20autistic%20people%20have%20intense,dinosaurs%20or%20particular%20cartoon%20characters.

Oliver, M. (2013). The social model of disability: Thirty years on. *Disability & Society.* https://doi.org/10.1080/09687599.2013.818773

Palmqvist, M., Edman, G., & Bölte, S. (2014). Screening for substance use disorders in neurodevelopmental disorders: A clinical routine? *European Child & Adolescent Psychiatry, 23*(5), 365–368. https://doi.org/10.1007/s00787-013-0459-x

Paode, P. (2020). Better data make better policy: Defining unmet housing needs of Adults with autism and other neurodiversities. http://doi.org/10.13140/RG.2.2.14233.03686

Papadopoulos, C., Lodder, A., Constantinou, G., & Randhawa, G. (2019). Systematic review of the relationship between autism stigma and informal caregiver mental health. *Journal of Autism and Developmental Disorders, 49*(4), 1665–1685. https://doi.org/10.1007/s10803-018-3835-z

Pathological Demand Avoidance Society. (2022). Identifying & assessing a PDA profile - Practice guidance. *PDA Society*, 1–31. https://www.pdasociety.org.uk/wp-content/uploads/2023/02/Identifying-Assessing-a-PDA-profile-Practice-Guidance-v1.1.pdf

Pathological Demand Avoidance Society. (n.d.). What is PDA? A guide to the pathological demand avoidance profile of autism. *PDA Society,* 1–14. https://www.pdasociety.org.uk/wp-content/uploads/2021/04/What-is-PDA-booklet-website-v2.1.pdf

Patra, K. P., & De Jesus, O. (2023). Echolalia. In *StatPearls*. StatPearls Publishing. https://www.ncbi.nlm.nih.gov/books/NBK565908/#

Paul, R., Campbell, D., Gilbert, K., & Tsiouri, I. (2013). Comparing spoken language treatments for minimally verbal preschoolers with autism spectrum disorders. *Journal of Autism and Developmental Disorder, 43*(2), 418–431. https://doi.org/10.1007/s10803-012-1583-z

Peña-Salazar, C., Arrufat, F., Santos, J. M., Fontanet, A., González-Castro, G., Más, S., Roura-Poch, P., & Valdés-Stauber, J. (2020). Underdiagnosis of psychiatric disorders in people with intellectual disabilities: Differences between psychiatric disorders and challenging behaviour. Journal of Intellectual Disabilities, 24(3), 326–338. https://doi.org/10.1177/1744629518798259

People with disability Australia. (n.d.). *Social model of disability.* Retrieved on July 24, 2024 from https://pwd.org.au/resources/models-of-disability/

Perry, E., Mandy, W., Hull, L., & Cage, E. (2022). Understanding camouflaging as a response to autism-related stigma: A social identity theory approach. *Journal of autism and developmental disorders*, 52(2), 800–810. https://doi.org/10.1007/s10803-021-04987-w

Persico, A. M., & Sacco, R. (2014). Endophenotypes in autism spectrum disorders. In V. Patel, V. Preedy, & C. Martin (Eds.), *Comprehensive guide to autism* (pp. 77–95). Springer. https://doi.org/10.1007/978-1-4614-4788-7_1

Petty, S., & Ellis, A. (2024). The meaning of autistic movements. *Autism*, 28(12), 3015-3020. https://doi.org/10.1177/13623613241262151

Powell, T., Parker, J., Kitson, H., & Rogalewski, M. (2024). "It was like the final piece in the puzzle for me": A qualitative study on the experiences of autistic women initially diagnosed with borderline personality disorder. *Autism in Adulthood.* Advance online publication. https://doi.org/10.1089/aut.2023.0031

Putz, C., Sparkes, I. and Foubert, J. (2021) Outcomes for disabled people in the UK: 2020, London. Office for Natioanl Statistics.

Radev, S., Freeth, M., & Thompson, A. R. (2024). "I'm not just being difficult . . . I'm finding it difficult": A qualitative approach to understanding experiences of autistic parents when interacting with statutory services regarding their autistic child. *Autism, 28*(6), 1394–1404. https://doi.org/10.1177/13623613231212794

Rankin, J. A., DiGiovanni, G. M., McKeown, E. S., Shah, C. K., & Brodkin, E. S. (2024). Incorporating self-advocacy and empowerment into small group therapy for adults on the autism spectrum: A pilot study. *Research in Autism Spectrum Disorders, 117*, 102425. https://doi.org/10.1016/j.rasd.2024.102425

Rautio, D., Andrén, P., Bjureberg, L., Silverberg-Mörse, M., Mataix-Cols, D., & de la Cruz, L. F. (2023). Body-focused repetitive behavior disorders in children and adolescents: Clinical characteristics and treatment outcomes in a naturalistic setting. *Behavior Therapy.* Advanced online publication. https://doi.org/10.1016/j.beth.2023.07.010

Raymaker, D. M., McDonald, K. E., Ashkenazy, E., Gerrity, M., Baggs, A. M., Kripke, C., Hourston, S., & Nicolaidis, C. (2017). Barriers to healthcare: Instrument development and comparison between autistic adults and adults with and without other disabilities. *Autism*, *21*(8), 972–984. https://doi.org/10.1177/1362361316661261

Raymaker, D. M., Teo, A. R., Steckler, N. A., Lentz, B., Scharer, M., Delos Santos, A., Kapp, S. K., Hunter, M., Joyce, A., & Nicolaidis, C. (2020). "Having all of your internal resources exhausted beyond measure and being left with no clean-up crew": Defining autistic burnout. *Autism in adulthood, 2*(2), 132–143. https://doi.org/10.1089/aut.2019.0079

Reuben, K. E., Stanzione, C. M., & Singleton, J. L. (2021). Interpersonal trauma and posttraumatic stress in autistic adults. *Autism in Adulthood, 3*(3), 247–256. https://doi.org/10.1089/aut.2020.0073

Rodgers, M., Marshall, D., Simmonds, M., Le Couteur, A., Biswas, M., Wright, K., ... & Hodgson, R. (2020). Interventions based on early intensive applied behaviour analysis for autistic children: a systematic review and cost-effectiveness analysis. Health Technology Assessment, 24(35), 1.-306. http://doi.org/10.3310/hta24350

Rong, Y., Yang, C.- J., Jin, Y., & Wang, Y. (2021). Prevalence of attention-deficit/hyperactivity disorder in individuals with autism spectrum disorder: A meta-analysis. *Research in Autism Spectrum Disorders, 83*(1). https://doi.org/10.1016/j.rasd.2021.101759

Rosenblatt, A. I., & Carbone, P. S. (2019). *Autism Spectrum Disorder: What every parent needs to know* (2nd ed.). American Academy of Pediatrics.

Routledge, F. (2024). *Exploring the self-diagnosis experiences of self-diagnosed autistic women* [Thesis, University of Toronto]. TSpace. https://tspace.library.utoronto.ca/handle/1807/138070

Roux, Anne M., Shattuck, Paul T., Rast, Jessica E., Rava, Julianna A., and Anderson, Kristy, A. National Autism Indicators Report: Transition into Young Adulthood. Philadelphia, PA: Life Course Outcomes Research Program, A.J. Drexel Autism Institute, Drexel University, 2015.

Rumball, F., Brook, L., Happé, F., & Karl, A. (2021). Heightened risk of posttraumatic stress disorder in adults with autism spectrum disorder: The role of cumulative trauma and memory deficits. *Research in Developmental Disabilities, 110.* https://doi.org/10.1016/j.ridd.2020.103848

Rutter, M. (1978). Diagnosis and definition of childhood autism. *Journal of autism and childhood schizophrenia, 8*(2), 139–161. https://doi.org/10.1007/BF01537863

Ruzzano, L., Borsboom, D., & Geurts, H. M. (2015). Repetitive behaviors in autism and obsessive–compulsive disorder: New perspectives from a network analysis. *Journal of Autism and Developmental Disorders, 45*(1), 192–202. https://doi.org/10.1007/s10803-014-2204-9

Ryan, S., Roberts, J., & Beamish, W. (2022). Echolalia in autism: A scoping review. *International Journal of Disability, Development, and Education.* https://doi.org/10.1080/1034912X.2022.2154324

Salleh, N. S., Abdullah, K. L., Yoong, T. L., Jayanath, S., & Husain, M. (2020). Parents' experiences of affiliate stigma when caring for a child with autism spectrum disorder (ASD): A meta-synthesis of qualitative studies.

Journal of Pediatric Nursing, 55, 174–183. https://doi.org/10.1016/j.pedn.2020.09.002

Sasson, N., Faso, D., & Nugent, J. (2017). Neurotypical peers are less willing to interact withthose with autism based on thin slice judgments. Scientific Reports, 7.https://doi.org/10.1038/srep40700

Sarris, M. (2015, October 20). *Measuring intelligence in autism.* Kennedy Krieger Institute. https://www.kennedykrieger.org/stories/interactive-autism-network-ian/measuring-iq-autism

Schippers, L. M., Horstman, L. I., Velde, H. V. D., Pereira, R. R., Zinkstok, J., Mostert, J. C., Greven, C. U., & Hoogman, M. (2022). A qualitative and quantitative study of self-reported positive characteristics of individuals with ADHD. *Frontiers in Psychiatry, 13*, 922788. https://doi.org/10.3389/fpsyt.2022.922788

Schwartz, S., & Moore, R. (2021). Ending segregated workshops and promoting competitive, integrated employment (CIE). *Disability Employment TA Center.* https://aoddisabilityemploymenttacenter.com/wp-content/uploads/2021/07/DETAC_BY_Resource_PA_Legal_Foundations_Pt_1_Final_508.pdf

Shalev, I., Warrier, V., Greenberg, D. M., Smith, P., Allison, C., Baron-Cohen, S., . . . & Uzefovsky, F. (2022). Reexamining empathy in autism: Empathic disequilibrium as a novel predictor of autism diagnosis and autistic traits. *Autism Research, 15*(10), 1917–1928. http://doi.org/10.1002/aur.2794

Simonoff, E., Pickles, A., Charman, T., Chandler, S., Loucas, T., & Baird, G. (2008). Psychiatric disorders in children with autism spectrum disorders: prevalence, comorbidity, and associated factors in a population-derived sample. *Journal of the American Academy of Child & Adolescent Psychiatry, 47*(8), 921–929. https://doi.org/10.1097/CHI.0b013e318179964f

Sinclair, J. (1993). Don't mourn for us. Our Voice, 1(3). http://www.autreat.com/dont_mourn.html

Social Security Administration. (n.d.). Understanding Supplemental Security Income SSI Resources—2023 Edition. https://www.ssa.gov/ssi/text-resources-ussi.htm

Sokolova, E., Oerlemans, A. M., Rommelse, N. N., Groot, P., Hartman, C. A., Glennon, J. C., Claassen, T., Heskes, T., & Buitelaar, J. K. (2017). A causal and mediation analysis of the comorbidity between attention deficit hyperactivity disorder (ADHD) and autism spectrum disorder (ASD). *Journal of Autism and Developmental Disorders, 47*, 1595–1604. https://doi.org/10.1007/s10803-017-3083-7

Spain, D., Sin, J., Linder, K. B., McMahon, J., & Happe, F. (2018). Social anxiety disorder in autism spectrum disorder: A systematic review.

Research in Autism Spectrum Disorder, 52, 51–68. https://doi.org/10.1016/j.rasd.2018.04.007

Spain & Happé, 2020Spain, D., & Happé, F. (2020). How to optimise cognitive behaviour therapy (CBT) for people with autism spectrum disorders (ASD): A Delphi study. *Journal of Rational-Emotive & Cognitive-Behavior Therapy, 38*(2), 184–208. https://doi.org/10.1007/s10942-019-00335

Stedman, A., Taylor, B., Erard, M., Peura, C., & Siegel, M. (2019). Are Children Severely Affected by Autism Spectrum Disorder Underrepresented in Treatment Studies? An Analysis of the Literature. Journal of autism and developmental disorders, 49(4), 1378–1390. https://doi.org/10.1007/s10803-018-3844-y

Steffenburg, H., Steffenburg, S., Gillberg, C., & Billstedt, E. (2018). Children with autism spectrum disorders and selective mutism. *Neuropsychiatric Disease and Treatment, 14,* 1163–1169. https://doi.org/10.2147/NDT.S154966

Steinbrenner, J. R., McIntyre, N., Rentschler, L. F., Pearson, J. N., Luelmo, P., Jaramillo, M. E., Boyd, B. A., Wong, C., Nowell, S. W., Odom, S. L., & Hume, K. A. (2022). Patterns in reporting and participant inclusion related to race and ethnicity in autism intervention literature: Data from a large-scale systematic review of evidence-based practices. *Autism, 26*(8), 2026–2040. http://doi.org/10.1177/13623613211072593

Sue, D., Sue, D. W., Sue, D., & Sue, S. (2021). *Understanding abnormal behavior* (12th ed.). Cengage Learning.

Sturm, A., Huang, S., Bal, V., & Schwartzman, B. (2024). Psychometric exploration of the RAADS-R with autistic adults: Implications for research and clinical practice. *Autism*, 13623613241228329. *Advance online publication.* https://doi.org/10.1177/1362361324122832

Szidon, K., Ruppar, A., & Smith, L. (2015). Five steps for developing effective transition plans for high school students with autism spectrum disorder. *Teaching Exceptional Children, 47*(3), 147–152. http://doi.org/10.1177/0040059914559780

Tajfel, H., Turner, J. C., Austin, W. G., & Worchel, S. (1979). An integrative theory of intergroup conflict. Organizational identity: A reader, 56(65), 9780203505984-16.

Taylor, J. P., Avellone, L., Wehman, P., & Brooke, V. (2023). The efficacy of competitive integrated employment versus segregated employment for persons with disabilities: A systematic review. *Journal of Vocational Rehabilitation, 58*(1), 63–78. http://doi.org/10.3233/JVR-221225

Taylor, L. E., Swerdfeger, A. L., & Eslick, G. D. (2014). Vaccines are not associated with autism: an evidence-based meta-analysis of case-control and cohort studies. *Vaccine, 32*(29), 3623–3629.

Tillett, J. I. S., Shivers, C. M., & Apple, R. (2023). Autistic perspectives of sibling relationships: Clinical implications for the use of quantitative measures in family autism research. *Contemporary Family Therapy*, 1–11. https://doi.org/10.1007/s10591-023-09679-4

Treffert, D. A. (2009). The savant syndrome: An extraordinary condition. A synopsis: Past, present, future. *Philosophical Transactions of the Royal Society B: Biological Sciences, 364*(1522), 1351–1357. https://doi.org/10.1098/rstb.2008.0326

Trew, S. (2024). Made to feel different: Families perspectives on external responses to autism and the impacts on family well-being and relationships. *Autism, 28*(8), 2120–2139. https://doi.org/10.1177/13623613231221684

Turcotte, P., Matthew, M., Shea, L. L., Brusilovkiy, E., & Nonnemacher, S. L. (2016). Service needs across the lifespan for individuals with autism. *Journal of Autism and Developmental Disorders, 46*(7), 2480–2489. https://doi.org/10.1007/s10803-016-2787-4

Turnock, A., Langley, K., & Jones, C. R. G. (2022). Understanding stigma in autism: A narrative review and theoretical model. *Autism in Adulthood: Challenges and Management, 4*(1), 76–91. https://doi.org/10.1089/aut.2021.0005

U.S. Commission on Civil Rights. (2020). Subminimum wages: Impacts on the civil rights of people with disabilities. https://www.usccr.gov/files/2020/2020-09-17-Subminimum-Wages-Report.pdf

Van Den Boogert, F., Sizoo, B., Bouman, Y. H. A., Hoogendijk, W. J. G., & Roza, S. J. (2024). Sensory processing and alcohol use in adults with autism spectrum disorder. *Alcohol, 114*, 25–30. https://doi.org/10.1016/j.alcohol.2023.08.005

van Heijst, B. F., Deserno, M. K., Rhebergen, D., & Geurts, H. M. (2020). Autism and depression are connected: A report of two complimentary network studies. *Autism, 24*(3), 680–692. https://doi.org/10.1177/1362361319872373

Vicker, B. (1999). Functional categories of delayed echolalia. *The Reporter, 4*(2), 7–10. Retrieved from http://www.iidc.indiana.edu/index.php?pageId=534

Voltaire, S., Steinberg, H., Garfield, T., Chvasta, K., Ardeleanu, K., Brown, M., & Shea, L. (2024). Inextricably tied: Nonbinary autistic individuals' views on how their gender identity and autism are connected. *Autism*, Advance online publication. https://doi.org/10.1177/13623613241257600

Wallace-Watkin, C., Sigafoos, J., & Waddington, H. (2023). Barriers and facilitators for obtaining support services among underserved families with an autistic child: A systematic qualitative review. *Autism, 27*(3), 588–601. https://doi.org/10.1177/13623613221123712

Walker, N. (2021). *Neuroqueer heresies: Notes on the neurodiversity paradigm, autistic empowerment, and postnormal possibilities, 78*(5), 339–341. https://doi.org/https://doi.org/10.1080/02604027.2022.2094194

Wang, R., Liu, Q., & Zhang, W. (2022). Coping, social support, and family quality of life for caregivers of individuals with autism: Meta-analytic structural equation modeling. *Personality and Individual Differences, 186.* https://doi.org/10.1016/j.paid.2021.111351

Welch, C., Cameron, D., Fitch, M., & Polatajko, H. (2021). Living in autistic bodies: Bloggers discuss movement control and arousal regulation. *Disability and Rehabilitation, 43*(22), 3159–3167. https://doi.org/10.1080/09638288.2020.1729872

Westwood, H., & Tchanturia, K. (2017). Autism spectrum disorder in anorexia nervosa: An updated literature review. *Current Psychiatry Reports, 19*(7), 41. https://doi.org/10.1007/s11920-017-0791-9

Whitaker, P. (2007). Provision for youngsters with autistic spectrum disorders in mainstream schools: What parents say—and what parents want. *British Journal of Special Education, 34*(3), 170–178. https://doi.org/10.1111/j.1467-8578.2007.00473.x

Williams, T. V., Hartmann, K., Paulson, J. F., Raffaele, C. T., & Urbano, M. R. (2019). Life after an autism spectrum disorder diagnosis: A comparison of stress and coping profiles of African American and Euro-American caregivers. *Journal of Autism and Developmental Disorders, 49*(3), 1024–1034. https://doi.org/10.1007/s10803-018-3802-8

Wilson, A. C. (2024). "Resist, reframe, redo the bullying, the lying, the harassment": A qualitative investigation of social anxiety and therapy as an autistic person. Autism in Adulthood. Advance online publication. https://doi.org/10.1089/aut.2024.0009

Wise, S. J. (2022). The neurodivergent friendly workbook of DBT skills. Lived Experiences Educator.

Wlodarczyk, J., Lawn, S., Powell, K., Crawford, G. B., McMahon, J., Burke, J., . . . & Litt, J. (2018). Exploring general practitioners' views and experiences of providing care to people with borderline personality disorder in primary care: A qualitative study in Australia. *International Journal of Environmental Research and Public Health, 15*(12), 2763. https://doi.org/10.3390/ijerph15122763

Yule, S., Wanik, J., Holm, E. M., Bruder, M. B., Shanley, E., Sherman, C. Q., Fitterman, M., Lerner, J., Marcello, M., Parenchuck, N., Roman-White, C., & Ziff, M. (2021). Nutritional deficiency disease secondary to ARFID symptoms associated with autism and the broad autism phenotype: A qualitative systematic review of case reports and case series. *Journal of the Academy of Nutrition and Dietetics, 121*(3), 467–492. https://doi.org/10.1016/j.jand.2020.10.017

Zeidan, J., Fombonne, E., Scorah, J., Ibrahim, A., Durkin, M. S., Saxena, S., Yusuf, A., Shih, A., & Elsabbagh, M. (2022). Global prevalence of autism: A systematic review update. *Autism Research: Official Journal of the International Society for Autism Research, 15*(5), 778–790. https://doi.org/10.1002/aur.2696

Zuckerman, K. E., Sinche, B., Mejia, A., Cobian, M., Becker, T., & Nicolaidis, C. (2014). Latino parents' perspectives on barriers to autism diagnosis. *Academic Pediatrics, 14*(3), 301–308. https://doi.org/10.1016/j.acap.2013.12.004

Zwaigenbaum, L., Bauman, M. L., Choueiri, R., Kasari, C., Carter, A., Granpeesheh, D. Mailloux, Z., Roley, S. S., Wagner, S., Fein, D., Pierce, K., Buie, T., Davis, P. A., Newschaffer, C., Robins, D., Wetherby, A., Stone, W. L., Yirmiya, N., Estes, A., Hansen, R. L., McParthland, J. C., & Natowicz, M. R. (2015). Early intervention for children with autism spectrum disorder under 3 years of age: Recommendations for practice and research. *Pediatrics, 136*, 60–81. https://doi.org/10.1542/peds.2014-3667E

Index

www.ingramcontent.com/pod-product-compliance
Ingram Content Group UK Ltd.
Pitfield, Milton Keynes, MK11 3LW, UK
UKHW020208290926
15470UKWH00001B/67